Praise for
There's No Room for Fear in a Burley Trailer

Pam's writing flows fast and funny from the page, yet her voice possesses an introspection and poignancy that makes you want to linger over every essay. She's a champion of motherhood stories, with an honest, humble, and hilarious approach, be it with directing and producing LISTEN TO YOUR MOTHER: BOULDER for three years, or her delightful and relatable writing. Pam's legs run fast, too. I should know because I ran with her once—for approximately four minutes.

—Ann Imig, founder and editor of LISTEN TO YOUR MOTHER

Pam's journeys have taken her through cross-country moves, intense race training, career changes, and the building of a family. As readers, we've been lucky that she's taken us along for the ride with her one-of-a-kind brand of honesty, warmth, and wit. Her pieces leave me often nodding in commiseration, sometimes laughing out loud and sometimes wiping away a tear, and always looking forward to the next one.

—Michele Vaughn, editor and author of *A Storybook Life*

Pam Moore generously and hilariously shares her stories in this engaging essay collection that will make your face hurt from smiling. Her voice is so genuine and her wit is so wry and self-deprecating that you'll feel like you're part of her inner circle. If you love good storytelling, you will devour this book.

—Stephanie Sprenger, blogger at Mommy, for Real and coeditor of The HerStories Project

There's No Room for Fear in a Burley Trailer

There's No Room for Fear in a Burley Trailer

And Other Stories

Pam Moore

Text © 2015 by Pam Moore

All rights reserved. No part of this book may be reproduced or transmitted in any form or by any means, electronic or mechanical, including photocopying, recording, or by an information storage and retrieval system—except by a reviewer who may quote brief passages in a review—without permission in writing from the publisher.

Design by Jack Lenzo

TO DAN
FOR BELIEVING IN ME, ALWAYS.
YOU'RE THE DONKEY TO MY PANDA.
I LOVE YOU.

Contents

Foreword by Joelle Wisler — xiii

1. I, Like, Totally LOVE Derek Jeter — 1
2. How to Move — 5
3. How I Procrastinated, I Mean, Got Ready for My Bike Ride — 7
4. A Three-Hour Tour… — 11
5. All I Want for Christmas… — 17
6. Bearly Prepared — 20
7. Just Gu It Already — 23
8. R.I.P. — 26
9. Pam vs. Shower — 30
10. SINEL LANDS AWESOME JOB — 34
11. Nu(vi) Love — 38
12. Extreme Bed Making — 42

13 "So East Coast"	45
14 Are You Going to Eat That?	48
15 Near-Death Experience	51
16 IronBoyfriend	54
17 Pam Goes to the Dentist	56
18 How I Almost Had a Nervous Breakdown on Vacation	59
19 Nuvi Love Lost	63
20 BOULDER MAN PURCHASES NEW CELL PHONE	66
21 What You Don't Know Could Hurt… Er, Really Gross You Out	68
22 Growing Up	71
23 And on the Eighth Day…	73
24 Regressing	79
25 Working from Home Means…	82
26 Feel-Good Project	84
27 Found This Week	87
28 Wishbone Waster	89
29 The Facts Ma'am, Just the Facts	91
30 The Case of the Missing iPod	94
31 The End of an Era	100
32 Creepy McCreeperson (a.k.a. Creep Depot)	104

33 Agnostic Maybe Starting to Think There Could Be a God	107
34 Thank You for the Lovely Fire Extinguisher(s)	112
35 I Get Lost and Dan Bails Me Out: Part Who-Even-Can-Count-That-High	114
36 The Blogs Are Scaring Me	119
37 Dear Dog Owners,	123
38 Farewell, Friend	125
39 The Yoga Scene	128
40 How I Make It Look So Easy	132
41 It's Happening	136
42 Note to Self: Learn to Read	141
43 Dos and Don'ts for Working from Home	146
44 He Said, She Said	150
45 Dear Guardian Angel,	152
46 Pregnancy Top Six List	157
47 Birth Report: Sweet Pea	159
48 Wanted: More Arms	162
49 New Mom Goes to Great Lengths for Alone Time	166
50 Notes from a Terminal Night Person	169
51 If It Looks Like a Duck, Swims Like a Duck, and Quacks Like a Duck…Then It's Probably a Duck (Where Duck = Voicemail)	171

52 The Unofficial YAY! List of Cool Things about a Five-Hour Flight Delay with a Baby	174
53 What If They Say My Duck Is Wet Because It's Wet?	178
54 True Story: I Met My Husband at a Bar	182
55 Home Alone	184
56 There's No Room for Fear in a Burley Trailer	186
57 A Day in the Life	189
58 What's the Deal with Park Etiquette?	192
59 Getting Back to My Roots: A Tale of Triumph in the Face of Adversity	195
60 Home Is Where the Mom Is	199
61 Fat Talk: I'm Totally Quitting…Tomorrow	201
62 I Hit a Turning Point in My Life When…	205
63 In My Next Life…	209
64 Mission Impossible: Waking Up	213
65 If You Ever Plan to Live with Me, You Need to Know This	216
66 Reflections	219
67 Just a Basement	222
68 Letting Go	226
69 Why Real Parents Don't Round: Air Travel with a Toddler	228

70 Traveling with My Toddler: Heaven Is Having My Lap to Myself	231
71 Why I Chose Home Birth	234
72 A Primer for Making Small Talk with Pregnant Ladies	238
73 No, I'm Not Pregnant with Triplets, but Thanks for Asking	240
74 The Bizarro World Golden Rule	244
75 It Gets Easier	246
76 Sweet Reunion	249

Foreword

By Joelle Wisler

WHEN PAM AND I met, I immediately wanted to be her friend, and that's what happened. We met in the hospital. Not because either of us were sick, but because we both reluctantly worked there—Pam was an occupational therapist and I was a physical therapist. I remember noticing her and thinking that I didn't know how it was possible that her tiny little frame could contain such a great big personality. Within two minutes of meeting each other, we had both somehow blurted out that we really just wanted to be writers.

And she has become a writer. While she has blogged since 2007 at Whatevs, she has also been published all over the place. Online, her pieces have appeared on Scary Mommy, The Huffington Post, In the Powder Room, Mamalode, Mamapedia, and Divine Caroline. One of her stories is anthologized in the book *The HerStories Project: Women Explore the Joy, Pain, and Power of Female Friendship*. In addition, as an avid athlete who loves to share both her fitness expertise and her musings on exercise, she is now a regular contributor to *Colorado Runner* magazine. And when she was pregnant with her second child, she spent hours collecting data, taking interviews, and writing a book on home birth. When I was pregnant, it was a good day if I could put on my socks.

One night, a couple of years after that fateful day in the hospital, Pam called me and said, "So, do you want to produce this mother's day show with me?" And I, not having a clue what she was talking about, said, "Sure?" Three years and thousands of phone calls, Google documents, laughing fits, texts, freak-outs, and blog posts later—and three sold-out *Listen To Your Mother* shows—we had done it, despite neither one of us knowing what we had gotten ourselves into when we started. It was Pam, and the show, that laid out the stepping stones for me to start a blog, to submit to things online, to keep writing, writing, writing. Pam has been my very enthusiastic, type-A, hilariously funny cheerleader the entire way.

This is a book about Pam's journey as she takes her own life by storm—from moving by herself to Boulder (where she knew no one and had no job or home) to her many exploits while navigating a passion to torture herself with exercise, to getting hopelessly lost (quite a few times, actually), to falling in love with a Garmin (and then her future husband), as she eats many, many questionable foods, as she struggles while becoming a writer, and, finally, as she becomes a new wife and mother. Oh, and the bangs. You'll want to read about the bangs.

Pam writes with a passion for life that makes you almost want to go bicycling with her if it weren't for her extremely poor directional ability. And she tells her story in a way that makes you feel like you were right there in the Dumpster with her as she tried to fetch her fallen lunch. Keep this in mind when you read about her home birth.

Pam decides what she wants and she gets it. I'm so glad that she wanted me as a friend. And that she wanted to be a writer.

1
I, Like, Totally LOVE Derek Jeter

LAST NIGHT I went to see *Into the Wild* at the Cable Car (this is a small independent movie theater in Providence where they have couches for seating). Going to the Cable Car always reminds me of my first date. I was sixteen. Said date took me to see *Pulp Fiction* at the Cable Car. He had seen it at least a couple of times and was excited for me to see his favorite movie. I was excited to get picked up by a boy! I only had a learner's permit. He had his license and access to his mom's Nissan Stanza, which was a stick shift. I thought this was very very cool. I wanted so badly to think *Pulp Fiction* was even half as cool as I found the whole car thing, but I didn't. Even having seen it one or two more times subsequently, all I can make sense of is a lot of drugs and liberal use of the f-word. Oh, and I enjoyed the soundtrack. I think I might still have a tape of it somewhere. But as far as the movie goes… I remember not being able to follow the plot and not having any idea what it was about. I hoped against hope we would not have to have a big discussion about it. Afterward, he asked me what

I thought, I said I loved it, we went for ice cream, and the film never again came up in conversation. The next day he called to ask if I would be his date to the Winter Ball. Success!

Less than a year later, I was dating someone else. One night he asked me what I wanted to do.

I wanted to see this particular movie they were showing at the Avon. I knew it was about something to do with modeling. He was game. I was quite pleased to be holding hands with my first real boyfriend during the movie, but I swear I was paying attention. So I did not hesitate when he asked me what I thought of the flick.

"I definitely liked it, but I found the plot to be especially slow... I mean, really, it was almost like there was *no* plot."

"It was a documentary." His tone told me this was meant to be an explanation.

"Oh, right, yeah..." I made an urgent mental note *LOOK UP "DOCUMENTARY."*

He broke up with me shortly thereafter, something about not wanting to be in a relationship. I wonder what could have been had I not pretended to know what a documentary was. Or better yet, had I actually known what it was.

Many years later, I was out with a Duke medical student. I was quite razzle-dazzled by his status as a future doctor. I would later find out he was pretty impressed with himself as well.

In an effort to impress the would-be M.D., I did some pre-date research. Although I knew virtually nothing about baseball, I knew he was a Yankees fan. I should have known it would never work from the start, being that he rooted for Duke and the Yankees, while my loyalties were to the Tar Heels and the Red Sox. The day of our date, I flipped to the SportsMonday section of the *New York Times* over breakfast. Derek Jeter had apparently done something no one had ever done before. I can't tell you what it was now, but I'm sure anyone who paid attention to this Yankees-Mariners game of fall 2001 knows the history-making play to which I refer. I read the article several times. I memorized the gist of the play. By the time the med student picked me up for the state fair that evening, all my ducks were in a row; I was wearing a carefully chosen supercute outfit, and I was ready to talk about baseball. As we started out toward I-40, he asked if I would mind if he just put the radio on for a moment to check on the score.

"Oh great, I was curious myself." I lied. We got the score. Emboldened, I continued the charade. "So how about Derek Yeter!?"

He looked at me quizzically.

I explained, "Last night? Against Seattle? Yeter caught that ball?"

"You mean Derek *Jeter*?"

SHIT. SHIT SHIT SHIT SHIT SHIIIIIT! I THOUGHT IT WAS ONE OF THOSE WEIRD SILENT Js. SHIT SHIT SHIT SHIT SHIT. JETER!?? YOU PRONOUNCE THE *J*!? WHAT THE FUCK IS THAT!? WHY DID THE *NEW YORK TIMES* FAIL TO MENTION THIS!??????

"Oh right, Jeter, yeah... I, um, just read about it and so I thought you pronounced it different... but yeah, Jeter..."

I wanted aliens to take me far, far away. Instead we spent the evening at the fair, partaking of a deep-fried Milky Way, getting dizzy on shoddily constructed rides, and peeking at the largest pig in the state of North Carolina. He said he would call. He never did. I did not yet know that if a guy doesn't call it means he is not interested. After much debate, I called him several days later. But not before pressing *67. After some chitchat he called me out.

"Where are you calling from?"

"Home."

"Then why does it come up on my caller ID as restricted?"

"I don't know."

"Did you press *67?"

"Nooooo" (pronounced with three syllables as in *hell-no-who-would-do-that??*).

I never saw or heard from him again, except one time at Lucy's (my then-favorite Chapel Hill bar), when I was really really drunk and accidentally fell off my chair, narrowly missing his freshly postoperative fractured ankle en route to the floor.

He was the last guy I tried to impress by pretending to know something I did not actually know. I was two for three. Enough was enough. I am not sure why I am still single, but at least I know it's not because I've been trying to woo men under false pretenses.

2
How to Move

1. Make decision to move
2. Fantasize about said move
3. Get scared, decide to stay put not because you are lazy but because it really is very good here
4. Realize you were just being a scaredy-cat and decide you need to go ahead with it
5. Freak out
6. Realize you are not the first person to relocate and tell yourself to get a grip
7. Make a plan
8. Be afraid the plan is not going to work
9. Poll trusted friends/family/anyone willing to listen on whether your plan is feasible
10. Go ahead with plan knowing you were going to do it anyway but still feeling relieved that everyone agreed with it
11. Be afraid you might jinx plan by even mentioning word "plan" on your blog

12. Post entry anyway but sleep with one eye open, just in case you have done something to lose favor with the blog gods, thereby actually jinxing plan, as feared

3

How I Procrastinated, I Mean, Got Ready for My Bike Ride

THIRTY-SIX-DEGREE WEATHER IS not the kind that begs to be ridden in. But alas, my off-season is over. I have been reading other triathletes' blogs. They say things like "Coach told me not to train for three weeks, just do some nonstructured activity during my off-season, and I am tearing my hair out!" My coach recently made a reference on his blog to his athletes who are so relieved to finally be back in training mode... He obviously is not talking about me. You know when you really don't want to run, so you fold your laundry, do the dishes, finally get around to taking out the garbage, then redo your ponytail eight times so it is just perfect before you actually lace up your shoes and head out? But then once you are five minutes into the run, you're glad you are out there? I think I am going through something like that, except instead of it being an issue of a particular run, it's the whole concept of getting back in shape. I was in off-season mode for so long that it started to feel normal, and now it's hard to get back into gear. Which brings us to this morning:

10:15 Alarm goes off (I told you I am still in slacker mode!). Immediately press snooze.

10:20 Get out of bed, but only because phone rang. Who calls that early!??!

10:30 Have breakfast, coffee, check weather, do some dishes

11:00 Consult pile of maps, book *Short Bike Rides in Rhode Island*, and cue sheet repository in search of new, interesting bike route. Decide in the end not to use any of them and to wing it.

11:20 Fold laundry that has been in basket for three days

11:25 Put away laundry from the drying rack

11:30 Decide legwarmers are torture and leggings over bike shorts are not appealing today. Feel it necessary to wear favorite Hind bike pants although they have had a hole in the left knee since crash in February. Must wear ripped pants, therefore must finally mend said pants, which have been in a pile near the sewing machine for eight months. Sewing machine + spandex = annoying project.

11:50 Pants are done. Change out of pajama bottoms and into bike pants which means am 5 percent dressed for winter ride.

11:51 Decide to definitely take new tri bike. Gorgeous, light bike's tiny frame has room for just one bottle cage. Plus, the aerobars are too far apart for the aerodrink to fit between them like it should. Realize that in order to have enough fluids for ride options are a) wear Camelback (not) or b) rid self of stupid good-for-nothing Profile Design drink holder attached to the rear of the saddle (although it is designed to hold two bottles, they invariably fall out. This product sucks.) Two weeks ago lost all flat-changing equipment going over a bump. Must attach new saddlebag from REI to carry stuff in case of flat and figure out how to attach aerodrink.

How I Procrastinated, I Mean, Got Ready for My Bike Ride * 9

11:52 Locate appropriate Allen wrench. Remove god-awful Profile Design rear water bottle cages

11:55 Find screwdriver. Attach new REI saddlebag

12:00 Gather two 650 tubes, CO_2 charger, two CO_2 cartridges, and one tire lever and place them in bag

12:05 Decide it is too annoying to go on one more ride with malfunctioning computer. Futz with computer. Attempt to remove battery, but fail. Resign self to riding without information about speed, distance, or cadence for now and remount useless computer display on the handlebar.

12:10 Set to work on making the aerodrink usable. Start by wrapping electrical tape around it to widen its circumference. Do this about thirty times, then realize will need entire roll of tape for it to be effective. Acknowledge need to find different solution. Think hard about what household object will solve problem. Find those adhesive furry things you put on the bottom of furniture so it won't scratch floors and attach one on either side of aerodrink. Go around with the tape a few more times. See if it fits. Add a few more sticky things and keep taping. See if it fits. Add one sticky on each side. Tape some more. Retest. It works! Secure with rubber bands.

12:25 Mix up three quarts of lemon-lime gatorade. Pour into 24-ounce water bottle. Pour water into aerodrink.

12:35 Check weather again. Dress top half of body.

12:40 Realize neoprene booties are meant to be worn with Speedplay cleats but am now using Look system, so cut out a bigger hole in the soles of the booties.

12:45 Put money, credit card, phone, eyedrops in ziplock bag. Realize license is MIA. Find it in jeans pocket and add to ziplock, then put it in jersey pocket along with a few gels and a handkerchief.

12:50 Pump up tires

12:52 Don earwarmer headband, helmet, sunglasses
12:53 Put on shoes, then booties, then change mind and take off booties, put on different shoes, then put booties back on
12:55 Get outside, decide its too warm for long-sleeve base layer, so run back into apartment to change into a tank top to wear under zip-up jersey
12:58 Departure

I didn't even want to go on this stupid ride, but I was damned if I didn't ride for at least the amount of time I spent preparing for it. I mean, really, how can you justify spending nearly three hours getting out the door then only ride for two hours? Although it was supposed to be a three-hour ride, I ended up getting home a little after five. [Insert *Gilligan's Island* theme here: "A three-hour tour…A three-hour tour."] What happened en route is a whole other story. Suffice it to say, I think being out of shape applies not only to actual fitness but also to all the crap that goes along with fitness. For example, when I was in Ironman shape, I would not have been caught dead dillydallying around for three hours before a ride! The night before, my water bottles would have been filled up and waiting in the front of the fridge, my outfit would have been neatly folded on my dresser with my heart rate monitor and chamois cream on top, my ziplock bag complete with money and ID would have been on the kitchen table. Sometimes I even filled my tires the night before. So right now I am just a little rusty, but that's OK because I'm not supposed to peak until September anyway. If all goes well this season, I will complete an Olympic-distance triathlon in less time than it took me to get ready this morning.

4
A Three-Hour Tour…

YESTERDAY I WENT for a ride with the intention of just meandering eastward. I had no specific mileage or exact ride time to shoot for, so if I got a little lost, I thought that would be OK. Since I moved to Rhode Island, a state notorious for poor or nonexistent signage, knowing I have the worst sense of direction ever and not being totally comfortable with the back roads, I have never set off by myself without an exact route mapped out either in my head or, more often than not, in my jersey pocket. Until yesterday that is. Maybe I was inspired by *Into the Wild*. I just read the book and saw the movie. The basic premise is a young man, Chris McCandless, hitchhikes out west for a couple years, then fulfills his dream of living in Alaska's backcountry for a couple of months before meeting his death. McCandless's tale was one of adventure. He lived his dream, to be free and unencumbered of material possessions. He lived for the moment. Like me, he journeyed sans map. Neither of us told anyone where we were going. I felt fancy-free setting off without a plan, on a bike that cost more than Chris's

1979 Datsun…Other than the dying part, I wouldn't mind living a little more like Chris McCandless…But I digress.

I got going around 1 p.m., heading east, over the red bridge, by Seekonk High School, out County Street, to Chestnut Street, passing through the farmland of Dighton and Rehoboth, reaching a familiar intersection around 2 p.m., and heading over to BikeWorks in Swansea, since I was right there, to see if they would have better luck fixing my cyclometer. The nice young man in the shop puzzled over it, but between the two of us, we brought the speed function back to life! He helped me get it from kilometers to miles and I was in business. [Sidenote: I have only had good experiences at that shop PLUS they have Bontrager carbon bottle cages and gel grip tape in all kinds of fun new colors, like lime green, lapis blue, royal blue, light pink, dark pink, etc. It's worth checking out; it could change the look of your WHOLE bike. Seriously. Plus, they had free samples of mini-sized Larabars.]

It was about 2:30 when I left BikeWorks. The November air grew chillier and the shadows stretched longer. I was a little pissed that I had chosen to ditch my long-sleeve baselayer in favor of a tank top. I knew, though, that I was about an hour and a half from home, so I wasn't too concerned. Until about 3:00, however, when I realized I wasn't sure where I was anymore, and the sun was noticeably lower. Shit! I convinced myself it wasn't time to panic yet. I still had plenty of time…

I alternated between pedaling hard, then going at a normal pace, realizing I might well be going fast *the wrong way.* You could say I was doing intervals. Around 3:45, I came upon a couple walking their dog and asked them if they could point me in the direction of Providence. The husband pondered while the wife looked at me asconce and exclaimed "On a bike!? Do you have a light?" Negatory. Like my adventuresome friend Chris McCandless, I lacked the proper preparations for my exploration. I had no intention of being gone after dark in the first place. Plus, I was supposed to pick my parents up at the airport at 6 p.m. Apparently I was in Rehoboth, Massachusetts. I took the kind man's directions and time-trialed it homeward.

For a while, anyway. Realizing I was finally on a familiar road, I got cocky and decided to take a shortcut. I went on this path growing less and less sure of my way with every pedalstroke. Every minute felt like an hour. The sun was sinking rapidly. My legs were focused on moving forward while I tried to keep my mind from spinning out of control with all the various ways in which I was totally screwed… I saw a busy road in the distance (something familiar?) and went toward it full throttle, only to be stymied by a cul-de-sac bordering some woods standing between me and the thoroughfare. A dog chased me around the circle… I escaped him but I was not out of the woods yet. At that point I crossed the mental divide between not being sure where I was and being L-O-S-T lost! I saw a man using a chain saw in his yard. I knew he wouldn't hear me even if I shouted, so I stood in his driveway, hoping he would look at me so I could get his attention. After waiting a minute or so, I started to feel creepy just standing in a stranger's driveway, wearing spandex and staring at him. But the more I looked at him, the more I feared maybe *he* was the creepy one, wearing plaid flannel and chopping stuff at dusk. I considered the ending of the movie *Fargo* and fled unnoticed into the dusk.

I pedaled like a maniac. Darkness began to set in, and my mind cycled between a few thoughts:

a) SHIT.
b) I'm SCREWED.
c) Don't freak out.
d) Will need a ride home, who can I call?

e) Cross that bridge when you come to it.
f) HAVE to pick Mom and Dad up from airport by six!!!!!
g) I'm getting cold.

It was now 4:45. The sky was turning shades of indigo and navy blue. The air was crisp. I was totally desperate, and I had no clue where I was. I came upon rolling farmland and a barn full of cows. I passed by a house with four cars in the driveway. I saw their TV was on, so they were definitely home. This could be a resource. I continued down the road and saw a couple more houses, but they held not nearly as much promise as the first one. I made a U-turn and approached it. Admitting defeat, I unclipped. I leaned my bike ever so carefully against a tree and stood contemplating my options. If only an SUV heading my way would stop and take me back. This was not a great plan, I knew... How did I know the person would actually take me where I wanted to go? What if they killed me? Or worse, what if I got separated from my bike? Hitching a ride was not my best bet. I decided the multiple parked cars at this house meant there was a good chance several people were present, thereby diminishing my chances of getting murdered. I theorized the chance of homicide was less likely with witnesses. My confidence bolstered by my hypothesis, I boldly knocked on the door. A little girl answered.

"Is your mom or dad home?"

A white-haired man with a soft, kind-looking face seated on a cushy leather couch craned his neck to greet me. A petite woman with lots of hairspray emerged from the kitchen. They listened as I explained my situation. It turned out the man was a cyclist too. He complimented my bike, which nearly made the whole debacle worthwhile. They informed me I was near Route 6 in Seekonk, right by the Showcase Cinema. Not so far from home, but even if someone was ready to come get me RIGHT NOW (it was nearly five), by the time they got here and got me back home there was no way for me to pick my parents up on time. How would I explain my lateness? I am the WORST liar. No parent wants to hear their daughter was lost alone on her bike at night, mapless, clueless, relying on the grace of strangers.

Sympathetic and impressed, they remarked, "Wow you biked all the way out here from Providence! What a brave girl!"

"I don't know… Stupid girl would be more like it. I really really appreciate you opening the door for me. I was really getting desperate."

I asked these lovely people if they would give directions to their house from Providence if I could get a friend on the phone to come get me. Of course they would. Before my cell phone was out of my pocket, a woman and her daughter, wearing matching horizontal-striped tops and jeans, entered the room.

The mom looked at me and said,

"You need a ride to Providence? I'll take you. I was just going that way. It's no problem. Where in Providence?"

"Well, Pawtucket actually, near the East Side. You'd really do that for me?"

"Sure! I live in Pawtucket too—that's where I'm going. I was just leaving now."

No. Way. NO WAY!!! This was unreal. The white-haired man reminded her she would have to take not just me but my bike as well. Maybe there is a god, after all, for this angel of a woman drove an SUV. Don't get me wrong—I am ideologically opposed to SUVs as a general rule. But she already had one. And she had to go to Pawtucket too. I will say this once and one time only: THANK HEAVENS FOR THAT SUV. I don't know what I did to deserve this. There's a chance it's related to the fact that I volunteered to babysit for friends the night before so they could go out child free. I think that's called instant karma? Or maybe there's someone up there looking out for me. It is astonishing that over the four years and thousands of miles I rode my bike in North Carolina, where I had no family, I never once got in a jam on my bike that I couldn't get out of on my own. Yet in Rhode Island, where I am surrounded by family, in eighteen months this is the third time I needed someone to bail me out of a ride gone awry. Is it a coincidence that this particular time, when my parents, my sister, my brother and my sister-in-law were out of town, a stranger extended herself to me? I don't know. She was a godsend. Are you reading this, Kelly? THANK YOU THANK YOU THANK YOU.

Not only did my bike and I get home safely, I had time to take a shower, and I was at the airport by six. I felt like Matthew Broderick in the last scene from *Ferris Bueller's Day Off*, where he's racing through backyards to beat his parents home and makes it just in time. Such a better ending than the one from *Into the Wild*.

5

All I Want for Christmas…

WHAT IS WORSE than your normal thirty-minute commute taking four hours in a blizzard? Talking about it with Channel 12, actually being ON TV, and missing the chance to see yourself on TV because you were outside shoveling the sidewalk so you could get your car into the garage when it aired.

One of my earliest memories is waking up from a nap and sitting in my crib playing *Donahue*. I was pretending to be Phil Donahue, and my stuffed animals were lined up around the bumper as my guests. Remember, this was circa 1981 and I don't believe there were any female talk show hosts at the time. As far as my memory goes back, I wanted to be on TV.

Twenty-six years later brings us to this afternoon. I left work and drove about five to ten miles per hour the whole way due to poor road conditions as the wet snow fell fast and furious. I can bike home from work in an hour. I think I could run home in two and a half hours. Instead, I drove home and found myself eleven miles into the fifteen-mile journey two hours after I commenced the trip. Stop and Shop was right on the way, and I needed bananas. I had decided to make banana pudding to thank my team in acknowledgment of tomorrow being my last day of work, however, I found myself sans bananas. This would not do. Although the Stop and Shop parking lot was dicey at best, the store was quiet, there were bananas aplenty, and the checkout line was nonexistent. Plus, I needed to stretch my legs.

Leaving the store, I found the Channel 12 News truck just two parking spots away from mine. What luck! As I scraped off my windshield, they wrapped up their interview with another shopper and turned the camera to me. My day had arrived. So what if my makeup was 90 percent worn off, and I was scraping my car with a flipper?

The reported inquired, "What are you doing here?"

"Oh, I needed bananas."

"You couldn't go without bananas in a blizzard?"

"I needed to make a banana pudding for tomorrow since it's my last day of work, but I had no bananas at home." (Duh! Doesn't everyone make a banana pudding when they are snowed in?)

"And what are you using to scrape your car?"

"Oh…a flipper! Poor planning, on my part… I really don't know where my scraper is… Last winter was so mild, and I was in North Carolina before that. But the flipper was in my trunk. I thought I was going to the pool, but I guess I'm going straight home."

"It's actually working, though."

"Oh yeah, this is innovation right here. I think Speedo has the patent on this one already, though."

They asked me what the roads were like, and I described what a nightmare it was. I hopped back in the car and excitedly called my dad to let him know of the possibility of my imminent fame. I considered calling everyone I know, or at least a few more people, but decided against it in favor of focusing on the treacherous drive.

At 6:10 p.m. (four miles and two LONG hours later), I finally dragged my wet feet and tired body up the stairs, opened my door, took my coat off, and started to head toward the living room to set up the DVR for the Channel 12 six o'clock news when my phone rang. It was my dad asking me if I'd seen myself on TV. He and my mom said I looked great on TV. *But I wanted to see it myself!!!* My parents were the last people I knew to get an answering machine or cable. Alas, they don't have TiVo.

My moment is gone forever, unless they replay it on the eleven o'clock news, which my sweet dad assured me they probably will. He understands what it's like to desire fame, regardless of circumstance. You see, this is in my blood. My dad was on the *Antiques Roadshow* last spring, and you better believe he hosted a pizza party for all his friends and relatives the night it aired. I feel my wish to be famous is as much a part of my genetic makeup as the fact that I grew to be five feet tall or that I have brown eyes. I am too tired to stay up for the eleven o'clock news, but I will drift off to sleep in much the same way I imagine most children do on Christmas Eve…knowing I was good most of the year, hoping to wake up to find trees blanketed in the purest of white snow and the treasures for which I have longed so painfully in the DVR queue…or under the tree. Whatevs.

6

Bearly Prepared

I LOVE GIVING presents. Shopping for my sister, for instance, is simply fun. Buying for her is a lot like buying for me but better because not only do I not have to justify the purchase, I also can feel good about it. Shopping for others, however, can be more difficult. But like anything else, when the mission is accomplished, you can feel good about having met the challenge.

Take my brother, Adam, for example. When it comes to hobbies and interests, I don't think we have a single thing in common. He watches football and baseball. I watch triathlon and cycling. He enjoys the water by paddling leisurely down the Saco River in a canoe. I prefer to put on my wetsuit and swim at Narragansett Beach. When we were little kids, he could navigate the entire trip from our house in Rhode Island to our grandparents' in Pennsylvania, a distance of 420 miles. I, on the other hand, couldn't figure out the two-mile route from our house to school. We do share reading as a common interest, although he likes graphic novels while I gravitate toward fiction. So shopping for him is tough, as I have to get outside my shopping comfort zone to search for things that would make him happy.

Over the years, I have come to the conclusion that what makes Adam happy is simply being prepared...for everything. That's right. Everything. You name it, he's ready for it. Remember Y2K? He had everything you could want in his basement, from canned food to water, batteries, flashlights, transistor radio, etc. If you look in his truck, you will find at least one blanket, flares, a first-aid kit, and jumper cables (among other bare essentials). When I moved into my second-floor apartment, he presented me with a fire extinguisher and an escape ladder. He is never without some form of cutlery, whether it's a Swiss Army knife or a Leatherman in his pocket. For his thirtieth birthday, I got him various sizes of watertight boxes, perfect for holding any documents or other valuables in case of a flood. (I think they were designed with kayakers in mind.) He liked this very much. For Hannukah this year I really wanted to find something he would enjoy.

My sister-in-law, Meredith, has said I am a great gift-giver. I feel this is one of the greatest compliments that could be bestowed on me (other great compliments include but are not limited to: you look thin, your stroke is looking really good, you are quite the climber), so I did not want to let anyone down. Moreover, my brother has a history of giving awesome gifts. I thank him for my adorable little digital camera and my brand new Garmin Forerunner 305, for instance. I have yet to finish making his wedding gift. He and Meredith married four months ago. With this in mind, I entered REI aglow with anticipation of all the Adam-style treasures and trinkets that awaited. To and fro, this way and that, I zigged and zagged my way through aisles of dehydrated food, bars, gels, Camelbaks, portable showers, and headlamps. I snaked through backpacks, bike helmets, and maps. Stopping only to try on two clearance-rack tops, I forged through Smartwool,

Coolmax, and neoprene in search of just the right gift. With the help of a kind young salesman, I finally found the perfect potpourri of presents to throw in with the old-school Patriots car decal I'd purchased online: an assortment of toe- and handwarmers, a book called *Learn to Play the Harmonica in 3 Minutes*, which included a harmonica (this was actually a gift for Adam and Meredith, hee-hee), and bear spray, which was supposed to protect you from bears or other intruders at a distance of up to thirty feet.

Tonight, after we ate dinner and lit the menorah, Mom, Dad, Adam, Meredith, and I took turns opening presents in our parents' living room. (Liz, we missed you!) As Adam untied the white curly ribbon from the gift bag, I assured him there was a gift receipt in the bag, just in case, inwardly confident in my knowledge that there was no "in case." This was a thoughtful, appropriate, clever gift for the man who is prepared for everything. He might think he has everything, but bear spray? Now this was unique! Seriously. Who has bear spray? I felt this would be on par with the beloved Petzl headlamp I'd given him a couple of years ago. Admittedly, I had an air of smugness as he unfolded the tissue paper encasing the bear spray. I waited with bated breath, sure that he would be thrilled with his new emergency-preparedness accoutrement.

He grinned, exclaiming, "Bear spray! This is great! The only thing is I have it already. You said there's a gift receipt in here, right? Actually, I have one in my glovebox and one at work."

If this were my movie, this would be the part where the music abruptly stops and everyone becomes suddenly silent. He has it? What? He has TWO of them???? Adam's reaction to my creative gift was met first with disbelief, then laughter, everyone shaking their heads, as if to say "Only Adam." All I can say is I hope I am with him when a bear attacks Pawtucket.

7
Just Gu It Already

I HATE PACKING. I hate it so much. "What makes you think you're so darn unique?" you might be thinking. "Is your apartment SO much more complicated than everyone else's!? Get over it!" you may say. But let me tell you what. For a self-proclaimed pack rat like me, packing might just be worse. A lot worse.

Take, for instance, the anguish I experienced upon finding a five-ounce packet of vanilla Gu while going through the pantry.

"You hit the motherload!" my sister, Liz, exclaimed.

Take it? Leave it? I was conflicted. On one hand, it was a perfectly good packet of Gu. Of note, my sister and I psychoanalyzed ourselves today and realized one of the reasons we both have a hard time throwing away excess (e.g., half-empty bottles of lotion whose scent you can no longer stand, an almost-empty bottle of SPF 15 CVS brand sunblock, a Carmex container with about two fingerfuls left of five-year-old Carmex) is that we hear our mother's voice saying "Why are you throwing away a perfectly good _____? I can use that. Give me that." My sister's best friend, Keri, was quick to point out that most people don't fill bags with castaways their mother might want, nor do they decide against chucking a useless item because they might later need it for an alternate use (e.g., you might want to use this scarf as a placemat someday).

After all, the Gu was a palatable flavor, vanilla being one of my favorites. It would really hit the spot if you wanted to fill your whole FuelBelt flask with the sugary gel for a long summer ride, perhaps. Moreover, it was given to me by an ex-boyfriend. OK, so he got it for free at work. In hindsight, I wouldn't be surprised if he'd stolen it (he was kind of a weasel on a good day). But still, it was a gift and I can't help but feel sentimental about gifts.

On the other hand, it was given to me two years ago. Also, I don't know where my FuelBelt flask is, and I always use PowerGel if I am going to be ingesting that much gel in one day. Plus, I hate taking gel from a flask anyway because I like to be consistent about my calories. Who knows how many calories are in a few medium gulps of gel!?!? I prefer to take 100 calories at a time, thank you. But I couldn't bear to put the perfectly good gel in the trash. I handed it to my sister and averted my eyes.

"Liz, please put this in the trash," I requested.

"Really? Are you sure?"

"Please, just do it."

"But what if you need it!? What if you're trapped?" Liz laughed as she said it, as much at the prospect of being trapped with only Gu as at the absurdity of such a ridiculous quantity of Gu in one mammoth package, but I think she was half-serious. Maybe our brother isn't the only one with an obsession with provisions for famine, after all…

Dang it. She wouldn't do it. I *couldn't* do it. That left one person. Keri answered the call. She was willing, albeit hungry for more information.

"Wait. You eat this as a meal?" Her eyes were wide, her expression incredulous.

"Well, not exactly as a meal, but you know, if you're out riding or running for more than, say, an hour, you need calories, so this is instead of actual food because it's easier to digest while you're exercising."

"Whoa."

Whoa. And in the trash it went—the calories, the expired fructose, the shiny, outdated butter-yellow and silver packaging, the memories, and all. And there you have it. A window to my maladaptive world, where a Gu is not just a Gu but a stroll down memory lane, an expired power bar is an item to squirrel away in case of famine, and a hand-me-down shirt you haven't worn in three years conjures memories of the person who gave it to you and visions of an imaginary time when it might come back into style. I must draw on all my resources (i.e., Keri) to get this job done before my lease ends.

8

R.I.P.

I'VE BEEN BUSY sitting shiva for about 50 percent of my wardrobe. No, friends, it was not just the expired Gu, mountains of Post-its courtesy of various pharmaceutical reps, and crusty old condiments that had to go in the move. I also had to take a hard look at my clothes. Or to be more accurate, I had only to hold up a garment and let my sister take a quick glance before she imparted her decree. Each and every shirt, pant, cardigan, pullover, skirt, dress, jacket, hoodie, and jersey was evaluated for retention in my wardrobe based on criteria including but not limited to: frequency of wear, whether and to what extent it was in style, whether and to what extent it fit, and the whim of Judge Lizzy.

Do you ever watch TLC's *What Not to Wear*? My sister played the part of the cold-hearted fashionista, Stacy London, while I performed the role of the pathetic guest, who shifts rapidly between angry defensiveness and utter mortification as London doles out unvarnished criticism. Luckily, I was spared the humiliation of showing the television-watching public the errors of my fashion ways. Don't get me wrong, though—it was really hard. All my clothes were on trial.

For some mistakes, I pleaded guilty without hesitation. Like the khakis I bought in 2003 (four years ago) and have not worn since circa 2005, or the really cute short corduroy skirt I got for $15.99 at TJ Maxx in 2006 and wore exactly twice. Some I tried to defend, pleading innocent with half-hearted conviction. I am sure a fancy New York lawyer could have kept them off death row, but instead they had me, the equivalent of an overworked, underpaid rookie public defender as their court appointed attorney... Cute halter-neck black polka-dotted stretchy halter top of my twenty-fifth birthday party, I'm sorry I couldn't let you stay. Liz said I hadn't worn you in a while and if I ever attended an event warranting your hooch factor I would be better off buying a new one for $14.99 at Forever 21... Trendy beige sleeveless ribbed top of New Year's Eve 2005, I bought you at Lucky Stars as my congratulations-on-finishing-the-semester gift from me to me. I'm sorry but I was defenseless. Liz said you were really cool...back in 2005. Keri crinkled her nose and said you looked like chair upholstery. I bid you a fond farewell... Old Navy girl's plaid pants, what can I tell you? You were a hand-me-down from Natalie, and you served us well. You made me feel skinny and hip in a Miami golfer kind of way. But the last time you were in public, Josh made a comment about my "pajamas," and Liz vetoed you without an opportunity for debate. I hope you will understand... And you, my mock-turtleneck navy blue long-sleeve wicking running T-shirt...we shared many a long run. You were my introduction to technical fabrics, rescued from Fleet Feet's sale crate in the fall of 2000. You helped get me to the start of my first marathon sans chafing, you let me wipe as much snot as you would absorb on your right sleeve, and you opened my eyes to all the non-cotton fabrics available to the modern athlete, and for this I thank you. The truth is we were over for a while, but I was content to romanticize about the past. Liz broke it down for me in no uncertain terms: Mock turtlenecks are lame, no one wears them anymore, and, frankly, I could not remember the last time I'd worn you. Good luck to you in your next life.

But I digress… Some clothes I tried to defend as not guilty on principle, like the gauzy white short-sleeve button down I wore a few times circa 2003, whispering "That was Memee's" (our late grandmother) as my sister ripped it from my weary hands, placing in the Salvation Army pile. Mostly she was ruthless. Sometimes she softened. The silky printed retro blouse was headed for the giveaway bag as I pleaded, "No, I *wear* that!!! Seriously. I wore it two weeks ago!"

I received a glare that said "You shouldn't have."

I pulled out the big guns. "Bubby made that."

The fashion dictator remained cool.

I went on, "It has a matching skirt. I gave that away. Please, it looks different on. I love that shirt." She relented, and it got to stay. On some matters she was willing to negotiate. For instance, between the black V-neck tank top adorned with sparkly stuff around the neckline and the brown sleeveless sweater whose neck was decorated with little white beads, she allowed me to pick one or the other. (I chose the latter. If you were at my sister-in-law's bridal shower, you may remember it.) Also, Liz stated all cycling wear is ugly. However, as a non-cyclist, she was not fit to make decisions regarding its survival. Therefore, instead of passing judgment, she simply stated that one needs no more than five short-sleeve jerseys and no more than six sleeveless ones. Fair enough. Eliminating my least-favorite obnoxiously bright polyester bike jerseys felt more like euthanasia than first-degree murder. I guess certain things, like a royal purple short-sleeve with lavender flatlock stitching or the Castelli jersey that only looks halfway decent on the skinniest of skinny days, deserve to be put out of their misery.

So it is with the utmost sympathy that I wish not just the aforementioned but all my old clothes a happy ever after. I have faith that someone else will find them at the Salvation Army and let them hang unused in a warm, cozy closet probably not much unlike my own. With any luck, I accidentally left a twenty-dollar bill in a pocket and am now due some good karma.

In lieu of flowers, please send gift cards to Nordstrom, Ann Taylor Loft, Banana Republic, REI, and SierraTradingPost.com. Thank you in advance.

9

Pam vs. Shower

I ARRIVED IN Boulder on Wednesday evening. I drove through Kansas that day. This was more boring than watching golf on TV and took longer than the wait time in an emergency room. Finally I arrived in Colorado and the landscape began to change. Hallelujah! I was even a little ahead of schedule. I imagined I would have some time to bebop around town before heading to my first appointment. I was to see one apartment at 6 p.m. and another at 7:30. I was waylaid, however, by a nasty snowstorm. About fifty miles from my destination, the traffic grew dense, the roads became slick, and at one point the snow was so blinding I had to pull over and take a break until the visibility improved. Argh. I just wanted to get there already.

I did manage to see both apartments, although I was delayed by about an hour. Finally I concluded the business of finding a home (to be continued the next day) around 9 p.m. My body thought it was 11 p.m. due to the time change. My mind thought it was 3 a.m. due to uprooting my whole life and driving nearly two thousand miles alone over four days. Well, not totally alone. I had the constant, comforting presence of my GPS.

Exhausted, I arrived at the door of the kind friends who offered me a place to crash while I got settled. I should state that I use the term "friends" loosely. To be accurate, the husband was someone I'd met on my Arizona bike trip the previous fall and had not stayed in contact with, up until a recent email exchange where I announced I was moving to his town and did he know anyone who needed a tenant or a roommate. I had never before laid eyes on his wife, his two daughters, or his two Lhasa apsos. The couple welcomed me graciously, showed me to the guest room, gave me a towel, and retired to their bedroom.

I longed to lay my weary head down on one of the half dozen fluffy pillows that adorned the guest bed, but first I needed a shower. The water pressure was superb. The warmth soothed my aching back. But all good things must come to an end. I turned the faucet knob and began to step out of the shower when I realized the water was still on but now cold. I turned it the other way. Now the water was still on and threatening to scald me. I experimented, turning the knob clockwise…counterclockwise…up, down, right, left, yanking on it with all my might, pressing on it directly, then from a 45-degree angle, to no avail. Anxiously I tried all my clever techniques about ten times apiece, hearing my own judgmental voice in my head, "You can't keep doing the same thing and expect different results!"

"BUT HOW MANY WAYS ARE THERE TO TURN OFF A SHOWER!? I AM DOING THE BEST I CAN!" I felt like shouting back to myself.

Ten minutes later, soaking wet and totally panicked, I jumped out of the shower, gave myself a cursory pat with a towel, threw on some pj's, and ran upstairs, nearly breaking the dog gate as I crossed the threshold of the staircase, hoping I could alert my hosts of the problem before they were fully asleep. I approached their bedroom, nervous and out of breath. There was the altitude to consider, but still, how relaxed can you be as you imagine yourself waking up the lovely people who welcomed you, a virtual stranger (at least to the wife, who, let's face it, is probably the decision maker), into their home to say, "Thanks so much for having me. Sorry for waking you up. I just wanted to let you know I broke your shower. Can you wake up and show me how to fix it?" I would rather have attended a Barbra Streisand concert. I seriously considered letting the water run all night as I crept toward their bedroom. I approached the dark hallway off the dining room, and I saw doors. Four doors to be exact. One was the bathroom. The other three were mysteries. I knew two were each of their daughters and one was theirs. Which was which? I had no way of knowing. It was like a game show where you try to guess which door is hiding a brand new car, except there was no new car and the consequence of guessing wrong was waking the whole family on a school/work night. I was not in a gambling mood, and something told me tonight was not my lucky night. I scampered back down to the basement and did what any healthy, normal twenty-nine-year-old woman would do.

I called my mother. She said to turn it off the same way I turned it on. Duh. That wasn't working. She asked me what I thought she was supposed to do over the phone. This was a good question.

"I don't know! I'm freaking out. I have no idea what to do."

She suggested I call them from my cell phone. This would surely wake them. I really didn't want to do this, but it seemed the only option. Neither of their cell phones were on, however. Now what!? My heart pounded in my chest as the sound of the rushing water echoed in the background. I entered the water heater closet. I looked around. I considered shutting off the water from there.

I realized I did not know how to do this. It was probably not a good idea anyway.

I felt a crushing sense of despair. I saw myself tossing and turning, unable to sleep with the sound of the water, dreading the morning when I would have to admit that the water had run all night and I had broken the shower. I could not let this happen. I had to try one last time. If I stripped every thread in that handle, so be it. I could not live with defeat. I faced the bathroom door and walked in with a purpose. With every fiber of strength I could muster, I leaned into that son of a bitch and turned it clockwise as if my life depended on it. My grunt was met with the sweet sound of silence. The mad rush of water ceased. Redemption was mine.

I called my mother back and told her everything was OK. And I knew, as I drifted off into a heavy slumber, parched, unable to fully inhale, in a town where I was basically anonymous, that everything would continue to be OK. I had conquered the shower. There was no battle I could not win.

10

SINEL LANDS AWESOME JOB

BOULDER (AP)— PAMELA SINEL was offered a fabulous position with Functional Solutions, a Boulder-based occupational therapy practice specializing in functional capacity evaluations. This position will not only allow Sinel to use her skills but also challenge her to develop new ones. The office is about four miles from her home and the possibility that there will actually be work is 100 percent.

Sinel arrived in Boulder on January 31, 2008, with an offer from a local home health company seeking to grow their Boulder County patient base, promising "as much work" as the energetic, optimistic occupational therapist could handle. Perhaps she was naive to accept a position that paid by the patient as opposed to a salary. Sinel admits "it was a bit of a risk," considering there was no written contract but that her supervisor "seemed so sweet and genuine" and that they "really connected during [the] interview." She recalls imagining the worst-case scenario, that she might arrive in Colorado and not have as much work as she wanted, that the job would require too much driving between patients, that the paperwork would be overwhelming. "So, the worst-case scenario more or less came true. But like my dad said, 'Hey if it doesn't work out, get a new job.' You see what your options are and you move on. I knew something would come my way even though the job I came for wasn't exactly working out." Records indicate Sinel saw one patient since she started working for this company on February 5. She was given the impression she would be seeing at least 20–25 patients per week.

Almost immediately, Sinel saw that her future with this company did not look good and started her job search. "It was disheartening at first. Of course there are always jobs for occupational therapists, but I was burnt out on the hospital setting, nursing homes can be downright depressing, and none of the outpatient clinics seemed to be hiring. I was beginning to think that I'd exhausted all the options in my field and I might do well with medical sales. I knew in my heart, though, that I would miss being a clinician and that sales just wasn't me."

Then she saw an intriguing post on Craigslist. It was a couple of weeks old, but she figured it was worth a shot and emailed her resume and a thoughtful cover letter. Within a few days, she had what would be the final of many job interviews last Friday. It went very well, and she was told she would hear something Monday. Sinel reported, "Saturday was fine because I stayed busy. I got out on a nice fifty-mile bike ride and shopped for a pair of Nordic skis. Sunday, I headed up to Eldora Ski Resort and had dinner with friends, but let me tell you, Monday was awful! By noon I was going a little crazy when I still hadn't heard anything, and by three I was using all my energy to keep from going completely nuts. I'm telling you, every minute felt like an hour!"

A watched pot never boils. While Sinel was enjoying a hike from Chautauqua park, her future employer was leaving her a crucial voicemail. They asked her to call back anytime tonight. Sinel glowed, explaining, "Come on! Like they would want me to call after hours to tell me they offered it to someone else? No way! I knew when I heard the message the job was mine!" Sure enough, they extended her an offer and exclaimed about how excited they were to have Sinel on board.

Sinel nearly bubbled over, exclaiming, "I am the happiest person on earth!" But will she miss being mostly unemployed? "In some ways, yes, definitely. I mean, how can you argue with not setting an alarm and going for bike rides at two in the afternoon? It's not all bad. But let's face it, a girl needs an income. And I've realized that it's important to me to have some responsibility and to feel useful in a professional capacity. And this position offers me everything I was looking for! I had basically given up hope that I could find a gratifying, challenging job that would allow me to be creative and use my skills—and now, here it is. I feel like the luckiest girl in the world."

Sinel's mother reported "I am so happy for [her]." In a text message, Sinel's sister reported she was sorry for not being more excited for her when they spoke on the phone but that she was very happy for her. Sinel reports her sister sounded sufficiently excited and that she wasn't sure what the text message was referring to but that she appreciated the sentiment. Sinel's father was proud and primarily concerned with the salary and health benefits. Sinel stated "They're good" but refused to comment further.

Is she afraid of jinxing everything by agreeing to an interview? She paused to think and said, "At first, sure a little bit. Who wouldn't be? But I realized my roommate Sofia was right when she said you create your own intentions by saying them out loud. It might sound hokey, but I think putting your intention out there and not being shy about it helps you put that energy into the universe and brings you closer to connecting with what you really want."

(Author's note: Sofia is not only not hokey, she is intelligent, driven, attractive, and funny. She is also single and ready to mingle.)

11

Nu(vi) Love

WHEN LOVE COMES, it brings a sense of hope, possibility, and promise for the future. It comforts you like an old afghan wrapped snugly around your shoulders and a cup of chamomile tea in front of a crackling fire. Its whisper is subtle but unmistakable, like April's breeze blowing through the windows, filling your home and heart with the spring's sweet scent. You want to shout about it. You share that joy with those who have already found it and wish that the uninitiated will someday experience it along with you. Liberated from the shackles of loneliness, you are confident you can accomplish anything you desire with your love beside you.

Or mounted on your windshield. So began my affair with the Garmin Nuvi 200. It started innocently enough… As they say, you always find it where you least expect it. This time, the place was a South Attleboro, Massachusetts, Circuit City. I hoped for a GPS device in my budget that would help me navigate the interstate highways from Rhode Island to Colorado. More importantly, I needed it to guide me locally once I arrived in the unfamiliar land of buffalo and big sky. What I got was much, much more.

I cannot say it was love at first sight, though. Although Garmin was the type I was looking for, I was skeptical at first. She had a tough time opening up initially... I struggled long and hard with the extra-thick plastic packaging. (Why do electronics manufacturers always do that??) And she wouldn't talk to me right off the bat. I had to be very patient while my Nuvi initialized. Only then was she willing to share herself with me. Even then, I admit, I was afraid to be vulnerable. I printed out Google Maps directions for backup, reluctant to trust her completely.

Quickly though, I began to see her for what she was—a beacon in the darkness. She became my guiding light. Ever supportive, she let me know I was OK whenever I needed some encouragement, directing me calmly and accurately. She gently steered me back on course when I got derailed. Like a good friend and confidante, she was my rock when I was adrift. How can I forget the time she helped me find a YMCA in Fishers, Indiana? Or the time she maintained her cool while gently letting me know a Bank of America was not to be found within a hundred-mile radius of Boulder, Colorado? Then there was the time I got cocky and thought I didn't need her and got lost on the way to work. Like a good big sister, she said nothing and got me back on the correct path with authority. Most of all, she offered me answers and security in a place where I was unsure of my footing. My Nuvi was my true north.

And I was not shy about singing her praises. For the first few weeks, anyone I ran across was informed, "This thing is a lifesaver!!!" or "I'd literally be lost without it!!!" Sometimes I would show her off, "Look, see you can just ask it for 'gas' and it will tell you where ALL the gas stations are in a ten-mile radius!!" Mostly, though, I was direct in my feelings, stating simply, "I love it." I did not know how I had lived without her. I knew only that I did not want to imagine a future without her in it.

But then I got used to her and started to take her for granted. As my friend Leah said of relationships, "The beginning is the best. It's the muffin top. The rest isn't bad, but you eat it because it's there." I suppose I grew complacent as the novelty wore off. One might say I was even abusive. Sometimes she would think I was trying to go home when, really, I needed to stop at Target on the way, and she'd say "Recalculating" as I pulled into the parking lot.

"SHUT UP!" I would yell.

"I thought you loved this thing," inquired my well-meaning friend and passenger, Natalie.

"I do! But sometimes it's so frustrating."

When I calmed down, I had to acknowledge the simple problem was that I failed to communicate my needs... Had I let her know I wanted to go to Target, my sweet Nuvi would have accommodated me without question. It was my fault entirely.

So I should not have been surprised when she left. I can't say she physically disappeared. I could still see her sitting in her familiar spot on the windshield, but inside, she was just gone. The first time I noticed was when she couldn't acquire a satellite on the way to drop off Natalie and Steve at the airport. I attributed it to the snowstorm. I just couldn't imagine that she really stopped talking to me. I wince when I think of how I made fun of her at this critical time. Apparently the last time we were really together was near Hapa Sushi... It must have been Saturday night on the way to Pearl Street. Sunday morning, no matter where I was, she showed Hapa with a star and a blinking question mark. Jovially Natalie, Steve, and I joked, "No, we don't want sushi, but thanks for asking. We're on the way to the airport!" In jest we mocked her, asking, "Rainbow roll? Miso soup? Edamame?"

This morning, I knew she was for real. The silent treatment was no joke. She stared at me limply with a look of Hapa and a question mark. She wouldn't even try to find a satellite. I went back to Google Maps to find my way to an appointment. My heart dropped as I tried to cajole her every way I knew how... I flipped every switch and pressed every button over and over to no avail. No matter how I approached her, she wouldn't speak to me.

I talked to a professional today. Actually I spoke to two. But no one could come up with a solution. We've agreed it's best to send her back and await the receipt of a new one from the manufacturer. I know I can weather the storm. I was OK before she came into my life, and, I tell myself, I will be OK without her. This gives me confidence. But it's still hard. I will have to be strong and find my way on my own.

Love is a tender thing. I abused my precious and now I am paying the price. I only hope I can learn from my mistakes and do better next time. I will not yell at her. I may even welcome her with a waterproof case. I know I will never take my Nuvi for granted again.

12

Extreme Bed Making

LAST NIGHT, A curious thing happened in my room. My boyfriend got in the duvet. No, not on the duvet. Not under the duvet. I did not mean to say he wrapped the duvet capelike round his shoulders.

He was actually inside of the duvet. On purpose. [Side note: For some of you gentle readers, this may hearken back to the days of yesteryear when my brother would place me inside unlikely coverings, such as a pool table cover or an oversized canvas bag; however, this was nothing like that. This was totally voluntary with zero prompting on my part.]

It began innocently enough. My white cotton Ikea duvet, fresh from the dryer, lay in a heap atop my down comforter. I hate putting the duvet back on, so I requested his help.

"Would you help me put my comforter in the duvet?"

I said "duvet" loudly and clearly, enunciating carefully, for I was not entirely sure he knew this word. Let it be noted that his vocabulary nearly puts mine to shame. He is our team's secret weapon at trivia night. (If he denies it, he's just being humble.)

He's a computer programmer for goodness sake. The guy is SMART.

So it wasn't that I questioned his duvet knowledge from an intellectual standpoint but, rather, from a practical perspective. You see, we are dealing with a man who feels a dresser is an irrelevant piece of furniture—why put clothes in there if you are just going to get them out again anyway? He favors a piles-on-the-floor method. He doesn't see the point of matching dishware. He thinks I am fastidious. (Yes, Mom, you read that right. He said that once!!)

Looking back, it happened so fast I can't exactly remember how it all went down. I think I remember discussing the approach and grabbing onto my corner of the comforter, but it's all pretty hazy. Before I knew what was going on, there he was, arms skyward, pinching both top corners of the comforter while the duvet rested tentlike atop his head and trunk. Without hesitation, once fully covered by said duvet, he dove forward and landed prone on the bed. He proceeded to wiggle forward, fully clothed, arms extended, supermanlike, until the upper corners of the duvet and the comforter fully met. I HATE when people sit down in their street clothes on my bed, but for these kind of heroics I made an exception. The end certainly justified the means.

He wrestled his way free of the bedding and emerged... proud? Relieved? Glad to be able to fully inhale? I wish I could tell you. In the thrill of the moment, I wasn't really paying attention to him. Rather, I was marveling at the state of my freshly made bed. I wish I had timed it. The task could not have taken longer than, say, thirty seconds, tops. My god, this was raw bed-making talent! He was a natural, for I suspect he'd had minimal, if any, formal training or practice.

I stood, jaw agape as he acted like he did it all the time. Like, no big whoop. NO BIG WHOOP!?

"That was so cool!! How did you know how to do that? That is totally blogworthy. Would you mind if I write about that?"

Permission was granted. If you have any questions, I would be happy to clarify the step-by-step instructions. I will never again insert a comforter into a duvet using any other method.

13

"So East Coast"

LAST NIGHT, MY boyfriend said I was "so East Coast." This "East Coast" comment was not meant to be a compliment. Substitute "East Coast" for "rude," "uncouth," or "uncalled for" and you will have a pretty good idea of the tone used in this statement.

Navigating through moderate traffic, I realized a little late that I was supposed to be in the far right lane. Alas, there seemed to be no break in the congested line of cars to my right. Prospects looked grim until I spotted my golden opportunity: right next to me there was about a two-and-a-half-foot gap between an SUV and a sedan. The driver of the sedan, a young woman talking on her cell phone, presented little threat of rapid advance, as she was clearly otherwise engaged. (Who said talking and driving was necessarily bad?) I seized my opportunity, jerking the wheel hard to the right as I slid into the desired turning lane at a 45-degree angle, simultaneously looking over my right shoulder, hoping to catch her eye with my hallmark "cute face." This usually works best on male drivers, especially when both parties' windows are open, but it never hurts to use a facial expression to say "I'm sorry,

I know I am cutting you off but really what choice do I have, I need to get in your lane, and you know I would do it for you." As I mentally congratulated myself on getting over before approaching the traffic light, Dan remarked on my East-Coastness.

What? I don't get it. What was so "East Coast"? If by "East Coast" he meant I am from Rhode Island, I just moved here, I don't know the area, I had to get over fast, and I wished I still had my Rhode Island plates so other drivers would cut me some slack, well, yes, I am "East Coast," thank you very much. This, however, was not what he meant. The Colorado native clarified his statement.

"I've never seen anyone do that!"

"Come on! You've never done that!?"

"No way!"

"What would you have done?"

"I would have put on my blinker and waited for someone to let me in."

"My blinker was on! Seriously? Wait for someone to let you in? You'd be sitting here forever!"

It occurred to me, much later, maybe Colorado drivers aren't as mean as New England drivers. Maybe out here someone would have actually been nice and let him in. This isn't Rhode Island, after all.

Come to think of it, one of the reasons I left the Ocean State was that people tend to be a bit harsh there. Cashiers at the supermarket don't typically look you in the eye, strangers scowl and look at the ground if you say hi when you pass them on the street, and they typically don't let you merge in traffic.

On the other hand, I moved back home from North Carolina in part because it was so…southern. Below the Mason-Dixon Line, I was annoyed with being referred to as a Yankee. At work, I grew tired of being eyed suspiciously by my patients once I opened my mouth. Inevitably they would inquire with faux interest, "You're not from round hare, are you?"

"No, I'm from Rhode Island, actually."

"New Yowerk… Ah thawt so. Ah could tale by your ayccent." What accent!? YOU'RE the one with the accent, my friend! I would resist the urge to tell them to look at a flipping map sometime, and go on with a smile plastered on my face, business as usual. If religion came up, I would just listen politely. A Yankee was one thing, but a Yankee Jew!? A good, god-fearing southerner just feels bad for a heathen like myself. In the Tar Heel State, I talked too fast and I was too blunt.

So in the South I was considered a Yankee, out here I am "so East Coast," and back home I was annoyed with the rudeness. It seems I can't win. I can, however, merge into any lane I want with minimal, if any, notice. My Rhode Island plates may be dead as far as the Colorado DMV is concerned, as they collect dust in the backseat of my car, but they are alive in my heart.

14

Are You Going to Eat That?

"ARE YOU GOING to eat that?" My boyfriend looked at me, astonished. I stopped, with a fingernail full of blackberry substance midstream from my ankle to my mouth, and stared at him. At first I had nothing to say. How do you explain to someone, "Oh, I forgot you were there, so I was picking some congealed purple stuff off my ankle and eating it, and I really wasn't even conscious of what it was until you mentioned it, but what happened was my blackberry yogurt fell on the floor while I was unloading the groceries, the container cracked at the base, and all the fruit-on-the-bottom goop exploded around my feet, and I thought I wiped off my ankles fully, but obviously it turns out I didn't."

I don't remember a time when I wasn't willing to eat just about anything. The drive was there when I was in elementary school, of this I am sure. I was sick and tired of the same peanut butter and jelly on rye, yogurt, trail mix, and Milano cookies my mom always put in my lunch. Everyone else's lunch always looked so much better... They had Cool Ranch Doritos in little lunch-sized packets. My Cape Cod chips paled in comparison.

Instead of Capri Sun punch (which is so hard to jam a straw into), they had Ssips lemonade or Coca-Cola. I was lucky if I got a prepackaged Little Debbie brownie. They had Ho Hos and Devil Dogs. I snacked on a room-temperature string cheese. My mouth watered instead for the canned fruit cocktail enjoyed by some of my classmates.

Things went from bad to worse when I was in the fifth grade. It was then that my mother delegated the task of lunch making; my brother and I were to be responsible for our own lunches from then on. Instead of blaming her for the monotonous lunches, I had only myself to blame. From 1989 to 1996, my lunch rarely wavered from a selection of Yoplait yogurt, Stoned Wheat Thins (and maybe some brie or peanut butter if I was feeling creative), an apple, and a couple of Milanos. I assure you, however, I was well nourished despite my bland lunches. There is something to be said, after all, for the prevalence of eating-disordered behavior among all-girl prep schools. You name it, it got passed on to me. I thank the mothers of my classmates for fresh turkey sandwiches on French bread, homemade brownies, fresh fruit salads, gourmet potato chips lovingly placed in ziplock baggies, and slices of leftover birthday cake wrapped in tinfoil. By senior year, instead of putting up unwanted food for grabs, more often than not the other girls would just hand me their food directly. If not for these castaways, I surely would have died, not of malnutrition but of boredom. I distinctly remember my best friend in high school remarking, "You would make a really good homeless person."

More recently, my best friend from graduate school took my position at University of North Carolina Hospitals when I moved to Rhode Island. She informed me that my former coworkers still spoke fondly of me. "Oh, what did they say!?" She told me I was remembered for having eaten a particular piece of pie. No one knew its origin or how long it had been in the communal fridge. I was not one to let minor details get in my way. I wanted that pie. "But there's mold on the crust!" my colleagues warned. Never mind the mold. I was content to eat around it. Why waste a perfectly good piece of strawberry cream pie? I enjoyed it but never imagined people would still be talking about the incident a year later.

So when I finally explained to my boyfriend that, yes, I was putting that purple stuff in my mouth, I also told him he shouldn't be surprised. Just hours before, I had told him the story of how I ended up lunging into the Dumpster face-first that morning: On my way to the car, I stopped at the Dumpster to drop off some trash and recycling. I tossed the trash into the receptacle and knew immediately something felt wrong—my paper trash remained in my hand. I had mistakenly thrown out my lunch instead! This was leftover penne, vegetables, and tofu, plus an apple, a tangelo, and grapes. And a great Pyrex glass container. I wasn't letting this one go without a fight. Luckily the Dumpster is situated within a fence. I was able to climb up the fence to get a little taller. This allowed me to peer into the trash. I spied my lunch atop some Styrofoam padding and tree branches. There was no sign of visible contamination, so, bracing myself on the edge of the Dumpster with my left hand, I reached down as far as I could with my right hand, successfully pinched the edge of my lunch bag, and reeled it back in. So I ate out of the trash.

It shouldn't be a real shock, then, that I was picking an unknown substance off my leg and eating it, now should it? Old habits die hard, I guess.

15
Near-Death Experience

TONIGHT, I ALMOST died. On a casual ride back from happy hour, Dan and I headed westward along one of Boulder's many bike paths. And casual it was indeed... I was hell bent on riding my road bike, but my black halter-top dress beckoned. Normally I would choose one or the other: dress + car versus jeans + bike. Today, however, was not a day for tough choices. Today I said, "Both!" So both it was. I found that the dress had just enough stretch and it was just long enough (knee length) to not be totally inappropriate for bike riding. It also was a good reminder to keep my knees together, which is good cycling form anyway.

I digress... We were about two miles from happy hour and maybe two or three more from Dan's place. I had just overtaken him. It's not really my style to be hypercompetitive. What sensitive girlfriend would elect to emasculate her boyfriend in broad daylight on a public path anyway? But I didn't have much choice. He taunted me. He literally dared me to try and pass him as he whizzed by me, tearing off like he didn't even know me. My only option was to take it up a few notches. It didn't take long for me to reel him in and then pass him. Which I guess it shouldn't have, considering I was on a road bike and he was on a mountain bike. [He insists I point out that I am training for an Ironman and he's sick. I don't know why he is so hung up on details.] I shouted "ON YOUR LEFT" with pure glee.

My glee was fleeting, however. Suddenly I was faced with DANGER. A peloton of no less than seventy-five people on cruisers traveling around eight miles per hour was coming at me head on. There were girls with tube tops on pink bikes with sparkly tassles hanging off the handlebars (oh, what I wouldn't give for one of those) and men in Spider-Man masks atop beach cruisers with baskets, shouting "Happy Thursday!" and "Turn around and join in!"

I was paralyzed by fear. The cruiser people were EVERYWHERE. I felt sweaty and claustrophobic. Boulder's open space was closing in on me rapidly, from all sides. I was all the way on the right side of the path with one foot unclipped (yes, I wore my Sidi shoes with the dress. My flip-flops were in my backpack), trying to come up with a plan but nothing was gelling. The only thing I could think of was to yell for Dan, who at this point had overtaken me and continued on. I remembered the time he stood between me and a big, mean, barking dog and hoped that he would forget about the fact that I joyfully passed him just a minute ago and show me that chivalry was indeed not dead. *Please, Dan, if you love me, just use your body as a shield between me and this gaggle of disorganized, crazy, probably intoxicated cruiser people,* I thought. I yelled "DAN! DAN! HELP! WAIT FOR ME!!! DAN!!! WAIT UP!!!!!!" My screams fell on deaf ears. He grew smaller and smaller in the distance, into a speck, and then finally his form was swallowed within the mass of cruisers and I could no longer see him at all. I was alone, upstream in a sea of cruisers. One girl nearly fell off her bike trying to avoid me.

I finally admitted defeat, unclipped my other foot, and pulled over to the grassy area beyond the border of the paved path and walked ahead to Dan. When I finally got up the courage to clip back in, we were able to take a right turn and get out of the path of the cruiser ride. The rest of the ride was uneventful, save for the fact I couldn't let some commuter guy pass us. I sped up and motioned for Dan to come along. When he found me at the next red light, he said something I couldn't really understand about why bother to make sure some stranger doesn't pass you… I am not even sure it was English. Something about me being competitive?…

16

IronBoyfriend

THE OTHER NIGHT when I was on mile eleven of a sixteen-mile run, my phone rang. Why was my phone with me on a run, you ask? This ironbrain thought it would be a good idea to run from Dan's, head south, then come back north, and end at my house. However, all my important stuff was at his place, so I stopped over around mile ten, put my bare essentials in my backpack, and continued running. My knees started to hurt pretty quickly, and my ego was already bruised. I was running up a hill with my backpack, not nearly done with my task, going slow as molasses as night began to fall. Dan's ringtone was music to my ears at this point in my harried journey. I picked up the phone out of breath.

"Where are you?" asked Dan.

[Gasping for air] "Running!! Still!!! Where are you??"

He named his coordinates and suddenly my hypoxic brain hatched a brilliant plan.

"You're on your bike?" I asked.

Affirmative.

"Ride fast and meet me. I am heading toward home on Twenty-First and I need you to take my backpack."

He readily agreed. Help was on the way! Yahoo!! Finally I saw his shadow and ran toward him with my backpack. He graciously took it and pedaled alongside me, homeward bound. When we got to my house, however, my Garmin read a mere 13.78 miles. Not the sixteen I was looking for…

It was dark, my knees hurt, and I felt like crying, I was so tired. Dan asked me if my knees hurt (like injured hurt) or just hurt (tired hurt). I begrudgingly admitted it was the latter. I was ready to call it a day, but he encouraged me to complete my mission. In the dark, we went on, he pedaling so slow he might as well have been on a tricycle, and I just hanging on for two long miles while he distracted me with interesting conversation. When all was said and done, I had eeked out 15.75 miles, thanks to Dan. Who I imagine is probably blushing as he reads this. (Dan, just pretend you are me for a moment and you will be really happy because you are the center of attention!)

17

Pam Goes to the Dentist

IT TOOK ME a few minutes to realize that my new dentist was different. The medical office building was pretty nondescript from the outside. But once inside, the first thing that caught my eye was the receptionist. Not the receptionist as much as her cleavage, actually. I'm not a pervert, but it was hard not to notice. Between that, her bright blonde hair, skinny arms, and all her bling, she looked like one of the women from *The Real Housewives of Orange County*. She directed me to the waiting area. On the coffee table, atop which I expected to see *Redbook*, *Highlights*, and *Sports Illustrated*, sat a copy of *If We Ever Break Up, This Is My Book* (which I found very funny) and *Encyclopedia Neurotica* (which I didn't get to look at).

Shortly, I was called into the exam room. Once I settled into the chair, I was faced with a flat-screen monitor showing the KBCO livestream (my favorite station). They scored a point for nixing the easy listening/soft rock. Once the hygienist began taking X-rays, I realized this was a very high-tech system; the screen alternated between the KBCO logo and images of my teeth. I was very impressed with the level of technology. Until I saw an ugly, bug-looking thing on my right front tooth. With horror I stared and said nothing, for there were bitewings stuffed in my mouth. I realized it was just the cursor and relaxed a little. I then noticed the bitewing things were not the stiff, paperlike things I was used to. Indeed, they were high-tech too. They looked like two oversized memory cards that you would stick in your camera, welded together at a perpendicular angle. I'm not sure if that description lends itself to an accurate visual picture, but all you really need to know is THEY HURT. They hurt a lot! What happened to the low-tech device of yesteryear? I wanted it back. My mouth was not meant to be filled with sharp plastic corners. Moreover, this digital bullshit was getting on my last nerve. Every time the beautiful young hygienist found she didn't get just the right shot, she had to do it over, which meant more sharp things in my mouth. Back in the old days, didn't you just hope they came out right? This instant gratification thing seemed to me to be highly overrated.

Finally the main show started. Enter Dentist stage right. Make that Triathlete, Road-Bike Racing, Professional-Triathlete-Dating Dentist. Anywhere else on earth this would have been perceived as some weird, wild, wacky coincidence, but not in Boulder. Actually, this dentist offers everyone in the Boulder Triathlon Club a 20 percent discount, which is how I found him. This is why I prioritized my dental health over the rest of my body. I still haven't gotten around to finding a primary care physician or an ophthalmologist. Or even a hairdresser. But I digress.

From our introduction on, everything was pretty normal. Until Triathlete Dentist started scraping my teeth. Again I longed for the old-fashioned torture device of my past. You know, that scraper? The one dentists operate by hand? It scrapes your teeth and makes your gums bleed but you know it's good for you? That thing is awesome. Triathlete Dentist favored some newfangled ultrasonic (I did not make that up) scraper. It was connected to a huge apparatus and it operated via mechanically generated vibrations as it scraped my teeth ultrasonically (or maybe it was supersonically; I cannot remember). It felt like alternately biting into an ice cream bar and sipping hot tea, and it sounded like nails on a chalkboard. I was in hell. Leave it to a triathlete to require all the latest and greatest gear. I can only imagine how tricked out his bike is.

Finally, I was liberated. I've never been one of those dentist-fearing people. Truth be told, I actually enjoy dentist appointments. I rarely have cavities, and I like when the dentist says I have a great smile. This time was different, though. For one thing, it hurt. For another thing, Triathlete Dentist said my dental health was good, but I don't remember him complimenting my smile. When you don't have dental insurance, a cleaning and an exam cost upward of two hundred dollars. Is a compliment really so much to ask?

I was not totally sure whether I would schedule a six-month follow-up with the receptionist or "call when I have my calendar handy." Until I was about to exit the exam room and Triathlete Dentist called from across the hallway, "Do you want water bottles?"

Did someone say free stuff? Specifically, free brand-new bike bottles that are totally mold and bacteria free??? Yes Yes Yes! The hygienist handed me two bike bottles with Triathlete Dentist's logo on them as I headed straight to reception to schedule my next round of high-tech torture, I mean, cleaning.

18

How I Almost Had a Nervous Breakdown on Vacation

DAN AND I camped this weekend in Chama, New Mexico, as our friends got married there on Sunday. No, the nervous breakdown had nothing to do with the fact that I was trying to get pretty for a wedding at a campground. That was a success, for the record, flat-ironed hair and all. (Ladies: I recommend placing your makeup in a tightly sealed Tupperware in the cooler should you find yourself in a summer/camping/wedding situation). I think it was well worth it when you consider the amount of points I have stashed away for later use. Just imagine the myriad situations where I might play the "I Camped for Gene and Vanessa's Wedding" card…

Anyway, I did what any self-respecting triathlete would do and threw a swim cap and goggles into my bag were I to have the opportunity to swim. It turned out our campsite was on a clear, calm blue lake, surrounded by pines and mesa views. Late Saturday afternoon, I decided to head out for a swim. I told Dan I would be back within an hour and a half and trotted off to the water's edge. I swam easily for meters and meters and meters. I don't know how far it was, but at the thirty-minute mark I decided to head back. I looked up to sight the shore every once in a while, swimming steadily back to our campground. Or so I thought. I knew I was swimming in a rough approximation of a straight line, but I was a little confused when I looked at my watch again. By my watch, I should be back at the shore within about three minutes. But looking ahead, I would certainly need a kayak or a miracle to get there that fast. I resigned myself to the fact that I probably made more of a zigzag than I thought and kept swimming. The closer I got, though, the more it just didn't look right. I didn't recognize any of the boats lined up on the water's edge, and I couldn't locate Dan. He said he would be reading in his camp chair on the shore, but I couldn't see him.

There wasn't much to do but keep swimming. The sun had gone behind a big cloud and I was COLD. I noticed the cove extended to a point on my right. I decided the cove on the other side of the point had to be the cove from whence I came, so I changed course. When I got close enough, I called out to a man standing on the point, "Is that Island View?"

"The island's over that way!" He pointed to the little island in the middle of the lake. I tried another tack.

"Which campground are you staying at?" I ventured.

He replied, "Brushy Point West."

Oh, Christ. Brushy Point West was seriously far away from Island View. I had to clarify. Maybe this wasn't as bad as I thought. "Is that this beach?" Affirmative. Shit shit shit shit shit.

"Can I use your phone?"

"It's back at the truck."

I hesitated before saying anything else, waiting for him to offer to take me back to the truck so I could borrow his phone. He said nothing. I got out of the water and started walking.

"You're one heck of a swimmer," he called out.

"Thanks," I mumbled. I was walking quickly but I wasn't sure where I was going. I was cold, wet, barefoot, wearing a bikini, and sure that Dan thought I had drowned. I had no way of contacting him, nor did I have a way of getting back to our campground. I knew I was about a five-minute drive away…at forty miles per hour, that is about three miles, which is about…a mere two hours of swimming, provided I didn't get lost. My eyes were brimming with tears. Calm down! You are a grown woman. You are not crying. Stop it!!!

Thanks to a healthy dose of self-administered tough love, I was now a functional adult on a mission. I would ask the next person I saw if I could borrow their phone. I approached a lady sitting at a picnic bench.

"Excuse me? Ma'am? Would it be possible for me to borrow your phone? I was swimming and I got lost and I need to be back at Island View, which is one campsite away, and I was hoping I could call my boyfriend and get him to pick me up?"

According to the kind lady, there was no reception, but she was more than willing to give me a ride. I accepted and waited patiently as she explained, "I just need to do this shot before we go." She swirled an amber liquid (whiskey? scotch??) around in a plastic cup and drew it to her lips as I tried to mask my horror. Hurriedly, she explained, "Oh, it's not like I've been drinking or anything… I just… I had already poured this and if I don't drink it now, then…then the, um, the ants will get it, you know."

What choice did I have at this point? I smiled and said "Oh, sure!" cheerfully, as if taking a shot before getting behind the wheel was totally normal. I just wanted to get back to Island View before Dan totally freaked out. It was an hour and a half since I'd left, and I knew he assumed I was in serious trouble.

As we ambled down the road toward Island View, in the distance did I see what I thought I saw?? My car? Coming right toward us???

"Can you honk?? I think that's my boyfriend!"

It was Dan, coming to fetch me. I jumped out of the car, thanked the lady, scurried to safety, and apologized profusely to Dan, who indeed had experienced a panic over whether I had drowned and how to proceed. Luckily, some other campers had been watching me with binoculars (yes, this is totally creepy, but I feel the end more than justified the means in this case). They watched every misstep (misstroke) of my debacle and finally called to Dan, "Is that your wife?" He told me he initially ignored them, not realizing they were talking to him. Again they asked if I was his wife, and this time he listened. Although he didn't have a watch, he'd finished his book, which in Dan Time means it's been a while. He had no idea where I was, and he was on the verge of jumping in to find me, and he was considering calling the Chama police or rescue. The binocular guys invited Dan to come have a look, and sure enough it was me. According to Dan, it was not long until he saw me get out of the water. It was then that he got in the car to come pick me up. Crisis averted.

On second thought, I might not play the "I Camped for a Wedding" card, for now Dan has the equally potent "I Thought You Were Drowning, I Freaked Out, Relied on the Kindness of Some Binocular-Toting, Potentially Creepy Men, and Rescued Your Cold, Wet Ass" card.

Lesson learned: It is not only important, when open-water swimming, to sight your destination but also to sight the place from whence you began your journey.

19

Nuvi Love Lost

SOMETIMES, AS WARMLY and gently as love comes, it leaves coldly, rapidly, leaving you feeling as though the earth has shifted beneath your feet. You shake your head in disbelief, wondering how this could have happened. Was I inattentive? Neglectful? Unappreciative? Unresponsive? You rack your brain, but try as you might, you can't think of a reason. Life has already shown you that sometimes you have to accept there is no reason. Despair and loneliness fill your heart, which has been smashed and strewn about in thousands of tiny shards.

At least it feels that way. Rather, your Jetta's front passenger window has been shattered into pieces by the trajectory of a large rock. You find said rock sitting smugly in the passenger seat, which is now littered with broken glass as if to say "When were you going to get here!? This place is a mess!" Crestfallen, you rummage through the vehicle hoping against hope your sweetie has been spared. But alas, she is gone. She has disappeared in the dark of night. Just when you were feeling safe and secure, wrapped tight in the comforting arms of the safest city in which you have ever dwelled…this.

You call the police and eat cereal as you wait for them to come. Two tall, clean-cut young men in uniform arrive shortly. You wonder why you must be one of Boulder's two crime victims this evening. This was supposed to be your night to relax, read, go to bed early. As you crunch on your Archer Farms multigrain high-protein cereal and soy milk, it occurs to you that fate had other plans. To the kind-faced men in uniform you open up. "I just can't believe I got robbed." They say you weren't robbed. Your car was just broken into. You nod and smile, knowing it's not worth arguing, but inwardly your heart is breaking. You were robbed of true love, the kind you don't find every day. The police make small talk as if this is a routine event and ask for the serial number of the stolen Garmin GPS.

Trudging into the living room with the Garmin Nuvi 200 box in hand, your mind wanders as the cops record the details. Sure there were hard times… Like when she gave you the cold shoulder back in March and you ended up having to have a separation period before you finally worked things out. In hindsight you realize you may have been too forceful, too gruff… Maybe you said too many vulgar curse words that time on the way to your first day of work in Denver a couple months ago, when she was just too tired to talk to you. It turned out she hadn't had any sleep, any food, really, any chance to recharge her batteries in weeks. But you didn't know. You were frustrated, running late, and lost sans map, and now you regret taking it out on her.

But when times were good, they were so good. You relied on her. You trusted her. For ten months now you had navigated journey after journey together. She stuck by you the whole trip from Rhode Island to Colorado… She pointed out the closest McDonald's (their coffee is quite good) and never made you feel guilty for leaving home or silly for going to a faraway place where you knew no one, had no place to live, and only kind of had a job. She helped you navigate this once unfamiliar city like your partner in crime. She was there every step of the way to Ironman Wisconsin. When you broke your friend's French press in Madison, she gently lead you to Bed Bath and Beyond, never scolding you for your lifelong propensity to break things in other peoples' houses.

And what did you do for her? You trusted the world to be kind to her. You left her in your car at night, albeit in the console, but her power cord was exposed, leaving her vulnerable and defenseless on a windy night to a clan of hooded hooligans. Would you treat your next love like this? The answer was decidedly no. The bigger question loomed large: Would you attempt to find another love? Maybe someday. For now, you decide it's time to be on your own for a while.

20

BOULDER MAN PURCHASES NEW CELL PHONE

BOULDER (AP)— TODAY, Dan bought a new cell phone. For privacy reasons, he asked that his last name be withheld. Due to factors that are not totally clear, up to now he has been using a Nokia originally purchased four years ago. While marginally functional, the Nokia had some major problems. Primary issues were the fact that it hung up on high-priority callers such as clients and Dan's girlfriend (Pam Sinel) spontaneously. It also held a charge for a ridiculously short time. This also prevented Sinel from contacting him or having protracted phone conversations with him, which were also severely problematic. In a private interview, she reported the phone was "stupid." She also made public remarks referring to the phone as "a fossil." She stated that it was next to impossible to see the phone's display, particularly in sunny weather. "It was really hard for me to help him dial any numbers when he was driving. He drives a standard, so sometimes I would be like, 'Give me the phone, I'll dial,' but then I couldn't even see the contacts or anything, and I would just have to hand it right back to him. That phone was so lame."

When asked why he waited nearly five years to purchase a new phone, the affable software developer simply shrugged and said "It still worked." At this time, however, he is the owner of a brand new AT&T phone. He refused to purchase an iPhone and instead decided on a Palm Centro. At this time, Sinel has entered in a few key appointments and has attached her picture to her contact information. She stated, "I honestly didn't think he would do it this year. This is a pleasant surprise." Dan was not available for comment on the Centro.

21
What You Don't Know Could Hurt...Er, Really Gross You Out

I HAVE A few vices. They include coffee, chocolate/cookies/cake/anything sweet except hard candies, although Werther's Originals are acceptable, really bad reality shows like *The Real World* and *The Hills*, and, the worst of all, reading blogs. What kind of blogs you ask? Mostly triathlon blogs. Usually triathlon blogs of people faster than me (that leaves my options wide, wide open), often those of elite amateur or professional triathletes, or any that are just plain old funny. I'm no bloggist, however. I am an equal opportunity blog reader. I am guilty of reading blogs that just suck. You know, blogs where the author doesn't know how to spell or use spell-check, doesn't understand how to use punctuation, and/or says things that are inappropriate? As one blogger of whose writing I am quite fond once pointed out, when blogging, one needs to remember that he/she is essentially mailing a postcard to the ENTIRE WORLD. Whether some bloggers don't know this or don't care is inconsequential, I suppose. Reading their blogs is like watching a train wreck. You want to stop but you can't tear yourself away. Same as watching *The Desperate Housewives of Orange County*. Just saying…

Besides triathlon blogs, I like to read anything funny and those that are written by my friends. But when you are reading stuff your friends wrote, you don't get to enjoy that fun voyeuristic feeling, considering you probably are privy to whatever their thoughts are anyway. That is definitely the case with my boyfriend's blog(s). For one thing, we spend lots and lots of time together. I tell him all the details of my life, everything from "I had to pee in another cup for work today" to "I feel like a sandwich from Dish" to "At 1:13 today, when I was at work, I coughed." That latter might be an exaggeration, but I am a details person when it comes to information. When I give it, I give a lot of it and when I get it, I want everything. Like, when people say "TMI," I shake my head a little and go "Huh!?" in my head. What even is that? Too much information? That's like saying "My raise was too generous" or "I finished that race too fast." As in, that totally makes no sense.

Anyway, I take it for granted that Dan shares everything with me too. I assume that he does, and then I get all surprised when I find out something that I think I should have already known. Like Tuesday, he told me he had lunch with his dad. After the fact. I was like, "What? Spur of the moment? Like, last minute, he just happened to be in Boulder?" No, they were planning it. Huh? Why did I not know this!? Was this really important, Dan wanted to know… I guess not. There were blogs of strangers I had to check anyhow. No, no, I conceded, this was not actually so high on the importance scale.

Despite the fact that Dan failed to inform me of his lunch plans with his father in advance, my trust in him did not waver. I could say at this time that I don't check his blogs as often as I should because I am confident that he shares his important, interesting thoughts and insights with me in person, therefore I should not need to go digging around on the Internet. The truth, however, is that a) He never updates his personal blog (although he did once since he met me and the blog post was mostly ABOUT me so I loved it). b) His tech blog—I just don't get it. It's about software. The only thing I get as far as software is concerned is that it's what your computer does while hardware is what your computer is. Also, sometimes I wish I did software professionally because it can be lucrative and you can do it in your pajamas. And finally c) I don't read his vermicomposting blog that much because it's kind of low on my bookmarks dropdown, but actually it is pretty interesting.

So imagine my surprise when I was checking the vermicomposting blog the other night and I saw a composting bin, your everyday, run-of-the-mill compost bin. Even though Dan doesn't always tell me everything, I get the gist of the important stuff. I knew he was composting human hair. I remember when he was going around to different hair salons this fall to obtain hair for this project. Creepy? Eccentric? Yeah, a little, but what can I say, I love the guy.

The wheels in my head started turning as I read the post and stared at that picture. I know that bin. I know that end table… But from where? His kitchen? No. Living Room? Uh-uh. Bedroom? OH. MY. GOD. That bin sits a mere three feet from where I sleep!!!!! Between my side of the bed and the wall!! GROSS!!!!!! GROSS!!!!!! GROSS!!! He thought he told me, he said. He swore I knew what was in that bin. Didn't he tell me? Um, no. I think I would have remembered that. He was sure I helped him slide it under there. No, that must have been someone else. That bin was not bothering me at all until I read that post. For the first time in my life…I think I get TMI.

22

Growing Up

I SPENT A week in Rhode Island with my family, this time as a woman engaged to be married. I wondered if it would feel different. Was I an adult now? I wasn't sure. I have been wondering for a while now when I would finally feel like a grown up. As it turned out, it didn't happen when I bought a townhouse. It didn't happen when I moved thousands of miles from home. It didn't even happen when I made a budget on an Excel spreadsheet and actually used it. Nor did it magically happen when I turned thirty.

So it should not have been surprising that on both legs of my journey from Denver International to T.F. Green, my theory was busted. I was conducting an informal science experiment (pardon the oxymoron), my hypothesis being that my engagement ring would surely add three to five years to my presumed age. As it happened, two out of two strangers sitting next to me in flight asked whether I was a student. Preliminary data collection therefore indicates that having a ring on the subject's finger bears no relationship to strangers' probability of assuming said subject is still a student.

Upon my arrival in Rhode Island there was much fuss among my family and friends around me and my good news. I relish attention, so I loved this—in between loving the way my new ring sparkled beneath the recessed lighting of my mom's kitchen, glittered in the smoky air of Twin Rivers Casino, and mesmerized me between sips of coffee at the Starbucks in Wayland Square. I am not kidding, the lighting in Starbucks is truly sublime.

I also loved having sleepovers with my sister in our parents' guest bed. This was decidedly not so adult. I tried very hard to get along with my mother the whole week. I imagine real adults don't have to try as hard as I do. I held my nine-month-old niece and said things like "Aunt Pam loves you!" in squeaky tones.

This felt sort of adult, if only because I grew up with an Aunt Pam of my own. I ordered wine with dinner at a nice Italian restaurant with my mom and dad. This was definitely more adult than the way I used to drink wine (i.e., gulping from a coffee mug, on an empty stomach, in my college dorm kitchen).

At first, I felt like more of an imposter than a grown-up every time I said the word "fiancé." And I said it a lot. As in, "My fiancé and I are thinking of a June wedding." "Do you have a brochure I can show to my fiancé?" "My fiancé has a bunch of mismatched, chipped dishes he's had since college, and he doesn't understand why we need to register for a new set!?!" I think I am getting the hang of it now.

Will I miraculously feel like a grown-up when I serve meals on the matching white dishes I have my eye on? Doubtful. Will it finally happen when I call Dan my husband? I have no idea. I am starting to think feeling grown-up is like trying to touch the horizon. I keep getting closer but never quite there. I suppose the only thing to do, then, is enjoy the journey, now with my fiancé beside me.

23

And on the Eighth Day...

TODAY MARKS THE eighth day of my phonelessness. As my forebears celebrated Hannukah, the celebration of lights, to mark the miracle of a drop of oil lasting eight days when their temple was destroyed, I am grateful for the work phone, access to Dan's phone, the Skype phone, and the email accounts that have sustained me for eight days.

But if the Jews didn't have to tolerate more than eight days in ancient times, then why should I? At this point, enough is enough.

The first day didn't really count as a day because I was busy sleeping and absorbing the shock of the situation. It was Monday, exactly a week ago, when I realized my phone was MIA—the brand-new fancy phone I had just gotten and entered all my appointments and events, to-do lists, and memos into but neglected to back up on my computer. Dan and I had arrived home from Moab via Silverthorne when I realized the phone was no longer in my possession. Silverthorne wasn't supposed to be part of our trip, but a snowstorm kept us from driving over Loveland Pass so we stopped in the funky ski town for the night.

Where I proceeded to puke my guts out all night, in our motel room toilet (which was not so funky). Maybe it's not so sanitary after all, to go on a group camping trip (including children, lots of children with dirty hands) sans running water. (Note to self: Bring Purell next time.) The next morning, we were welcomed by sunshine, dry roads, and a substantially less queasy feeling in my stomach. We had completed the journey back to Boulder when I realized my phone was missing. I promptly called the Silver Inn, where the kind Tom confirmed my phone was there and he would send it to me today. I thought surely I would have it Wednesday at the latest.

Tuesday, Dan was gone all day for a course. It figures. On any normal day he would work from home (read: I would have access to his phone) but not this week. No worries, though. Dan's computer has a Skype phone.

Wednesday, Dan left again for his class in the wee hours of the morning (OK, 7 a.m.), and I eventually got up and went about my business. Except for any that involved the phone. Skype kept on telling me "Skype cannot hear you talking." I screamed and yelled some things that are not appropriate, but Skype still couldn't hear me. Neither could anyone I was trying to reach. Dan came home and patiently explained that the Skype headphone has to be completely plugged into the computer in order to function.

Thursday, I awoke to a new day, fresh with hope. As I rubbed the sleep from my eyes, I turned on Dan's computer. It wanted his Skype password. Skype password!? He didn't leave me the password! I knew I shouldn't even guess. You see, Dan is not a normal person who uses his favorite food or sports trivia (he doesn't even like sports) for a password. No, he is a special sort of person who uses a computer program to give him encrypted twenty-five-character passwords that I don't think he even knows what they are. So I told Skype to please email me my password. Which went to Dan's work email account. Which I did not know the password for. Or how to even run. Foiled again.

Finally, Dan came home (read: Dan's phone was available to me) and I was able to call Tom at the Silver Inn to get the tracking number for the phone. But he wasn't working. I frantically explained the urgent phone situation to the lady there who gave me Tom's number. I left Tom a message. He called back and gave me the tracking number. The USPS website said it had been delivered. Twice. Nuh-uh! I never saw it! I tried to call USPS. They were not home. Dan cheerfully pointed out "We have a tracking number! That's good!" I glared at him. There were only four words that could have made me happy: Here is your phone. Dan tried again later, in the car on the way to the rock gym. "It really sucks that you don't have your phone! Damn it!" with a tone as genuine as that of a game show host. It was sweet of him to try and console me, but he could not win. I told him we should just stop talking about it. Then his phone rang and he answered it. I accused him of trying to make me jealous. And so began my descent toward madness.

Friday, at work, I called the post office. They told me the phone had been returned to sender. Returned to sender!? But that made no sense!? Was it too late? Could its route be reversed? Don't return to sender!! Sendee is here waiting for said phone!!! NOOOOOO!! The post office man calmly interrupted me and said, "Ma'am. Ma'am. Ma'am." Really, he said "ma'am" three times. I wonder if that is how they soothe crazy people when they are flailing their limbs all around while the police try to cuff them. I stopped talking and apologized. He said it was being returned to Silverthorne and there was nothing else he could do for me. So I called my boy Tom and explained the situation, that perhaps he did not write the address completely correctly, and when he gets it can he please send it to me again, asap, and so sorry for the inconvenience. He promised he would. As it turned out, he himself had recently lost his phone and all his contacts. "Hey, that's a good way to weed out all the friends you don't like," I joked. He laughed. We totally bonded. I was confident Tom had what it took to get my phone back safe and sound.

The weekend was manageable, save for a work scheduling mix-up, which was largely the result of my not having access to my calendar. But otherwise, I was starting to feel liberated by not having a phone. Also, Dan went on a camping trip Saturday and left his phone in my possession for the week.

Monday (today), I checked the tracking number online. On the seventeenth the phone had been delivered to the sender. So where was it now? Had Tom sent it back again? Did it have a new tracking number? I had so many unanswered questions. I called the trusty Silver Inn but was informed that Tom would not be working till tomorrow. I then went through the phone's call log to try and find Tom's cell. I called every 970 number in there. (Why were there so darn many? Dan, do we know that many people on the Western Slope?) None of the people at the numbers I called knew anything about Tom. How could they all be wrong numbers? My brain was filled with question marks. A few hours later, I got a call from a 970 number. I told my friends to please excuse me. I took the call.

"This is Pam."

"Oh…I think…"

"Hello?"

"I think this is the wrong number…"

"IS THIS TOM?"

"Yeah, I…"

"TOM FROM THE SILVER INN? THIS IS PAM. ABOUT THE PHONE?"

"Oh, I just saw this number on the caller ID of all my phones." Tom sounded stoned.

"Yeah, Tom, hi. I was calling about my phone? That I left at the Silver Inn? Remember?"

"It's really weird that you haven't gotten it."

His tone was exhausted and annoyed. This did not seem good. I tried to jog his memory, to bring us back to the happy time we shared, when he promised he'd send it back to me. When we had a moment as he recalled how much it sucked to lose his phone recently. I pressed on.

"I know, but remember we talked Friday, and I told you it was going to be returned to sender and you said you'd get it to me? Did you get it? The tracking info says it arrived Friday."

He mumbled something about not having seen it. Oh, god. Tom, stay with me, buddy.

"Have you been to the place where it was being mailed since Friday?"

I heard something barely coherent about how weird this was and he was going to his P.O. box soon. I then realized I was talking to someone who lives in a mountain town during the off-season on 4/20. This was not seeming good at all.

"Tom, but you'll go to the P.O. box tomorrow and check on it? Right? I know this is so annoying. I will pay you. I feel really bad about this. But I really appreciate it."

"Yeah, this is…so weird…you know." Yes, Tom, I know this is weird, I KNOW, BUT DON'T LEAVE ME STRANDED LIKE THIS!!!! PLEASE TOM YOU'RE ALL I HAVE.

In the end, I think Tom agreed to check the P.O. box and mail it to me at Dan's, this time (I think) c/o fiancé Dan (apparently the mix-up may have been because he left this crucial line off the address), and I have in the meantime alerted the mail carrier that I am staying here. (Of course, I could get my mail at my own domicile but that would mean I would have to go there, and I am not in the mood.)

I hope the phone comes soon. I don't know how much more I can take. Tomorrow will be Day Nine. Even God rested on the seventh day.

24

Regressing

THE OTHER DAY, as Dan was helping me carry my hanging clothes into my new apartment, I was regaling him with tales of my yard-saling adventures.

"Oh, and beside all the housewares I got at the estate sale for five bucks, wait till you see the sweet-ass garbage can I found! It was only a dollar!"

I was grinning from ear to ear. My grin slowly faded, though, as Dan jolted me back to reality.

"Sweet-ass garbage can? Pam, seriously."

I tried to hold my ground.

"No, it is a great garbage can! Because the thing of it is, I would have had to pay like $11.99 for it at Target, but I got a great garbage can, you know, a tall one, for the kitchen? For just a dollar!"

Even I was having trouble convincing myself.

When did I become so cheap anyway?

There is a fine line between cheap and frugal and I believe I am straddling it ever so precariously. At best. The garbage can exchange took place only about fifteen minutes after The Great Bookshelf Find. Driving back from my old place, my car was loaded with the final load of clothes, a random assortment of foodstuffs, and our bikes on the roof rack. After a fifty-mile bike ride and one final schlep of my stuff, we were ready to get clean and get fed. First however, I had to make a U-turn to fully inspect the Great Bookshelf. It was sitting on the curb next to a matching desk in all its fake birch veneer glory. The matching desk I could do without, but the shelf was perfect for the spot right next to the fireplace! It was wobbly, but it had five good shelves. And as Dan pointed out, it was nothing a few nails couldn't fix. I had a hammer! I had nails! Perfect!!

"Dan, can you believe this! This is the Perfect Bookshelf!"

Enter reality, stage right.

"Pam, you're thirty. You're engaged. The Bookshelf is not that great."

"OK, but when we unload the car, let's come right back for The Bookshelf!"

Try as I might, it is hard to ignore the facts. I am afraid my standard of living has taken a nosedive of late. If you were to put my housing situations on a line graph, you would see a gradual increase from 2000 to 2006, then a plateau to 2008, and then a sharp decline from 2008 to present, where it is again at a plateau. My carpet has stains. My freezer has no shelf. The sliding screen door to the patio does not slide. You can only access my parking spot via a long alley that has two potholes the size of California. The laundry is outside my unit. This would be grand if I was living in Manhattan. Which I'm not.

Boulder is no big city but I will say I have everything I need within walking distance. Within ten minutes I can walk to Dan's, the Brewing Market, Jo-Ann Fabrics, Performance Bicycle, LiquorMart, US Bank, the Boulder Public Library, and even

Triathlete Dentist. My neighborhood is rife with lazy college students who leave all their stuff around the Dumpster instead of packing it up or taking it to the Salvation Army before they move. I ought to send them a thank-you note. This weekend, within mere steps of my parking spot, I found two Stephen King books (I might read them when I am done with every magazine, catalog, and article of junk mail in my apartment if the library is inaccessible and Amazon.com goes under), one Paulo Coelho book (I truly might read this one), yet another perfect garbage can (designated for my paper recycling), and a plastic bin (perfect on top of the fridge).

Sadly, I never was able to add The Bookshelf to my collection of Cheap or Free Stuff I Found on the Street. Eventually Dan came back, but he was empty-handed. Although we had "hid" The Bookshelf behind a fence so no one else could claim my treasure before we came back to retrieve it, the plan backfired. We left The Bookshelf dangerously close to the Dumpster, which made someone think it was…trash. So it was a little wobbly and it was probably from Target circa 1999, but why do people have to go around playing god, like they get to decide what's trash and what isn't? People need to mind their own business. Anyway, Dan said he saw The Bookshelf peeking out of the Dumpster and he didn't think it was worth diving in for it. Which I totally understood. I do have standards after all. Like, when I saw massive rolls of dirty old used carpeting by the Dumpster on Friday, I totally did not take them.

25

Working from Home Means...

YOU DON'T BLOG as much as you want because...

a) You are sick of being in front of the computer but more often
b) You haven't worked enough today/this week/period to justify taking a large chunk of time (as it takes a shockingly long time to write a post that takes two minutes to read) to do something other than work.
Even though
c) If you added up all the five-plus-minutes chunks of time you spent reading email/replying to one urgent email/checking Facebook/checking Craigslist/checking the weather/checking your bank account online/getting a snack/going to the bathroom/reading blogs, you know you would have enough time to write a blog post, for crying out loud.
While
d) Ironically, working from home actually increases the urgency of all of the above. What used to be the casual perusal of Craigslist evolves into an urgent pressing need to CHECK

ON THINGS when working from home. All kinds of things (furniture, apartments, jobs) because THEY MIGHT NOT BE THERE TOMORROW. Not that you are necessarily looking for said furniture, apartments, or jobs. You just want to know what's out there.

Right now, working from home means YOUR WEDDING DRESS IS IN A BOX ON THE LIVING ROOM FLOOR. Said box is TAPED SHUT. In other words, it arrived in the mail today and if you open the box, you will see the dress. When you see the dress, you will touch the dress. Once you feel the dress, you will have to put it on. And even though it's still a foot too long and the chest is way too loose, you will prance around like a pretty princess. Then you will try on your pretty pink heels and turn on some music (probably Madonna) and dance till god knows when. And then no work will happen. Which it desperately needs to.

So you finally decide that if you aren't going to be working for the next ten to fifteen minutes, it's better to publicly vent about how hard it is to work from home than to dance in said bridal gown till the sky grows dark. And you try to remember how lucky you are to have a job, period, while your wedding dress is practically banging on the cardboard box, begging you to let her out.

26

Feel-Good Project

DO YOU WANT to feel good? Here's what you do.

Find all the old stuff that, if you are a normal person, is probably in your parents' garage/attic/basement or your old room. Unless you are like me and your old room became your sister's room, which is now the yoga/granddaughter room, and your parents made you take back all of your stuff in a way that was nonnegotiable—in other words they paid to have all that stuff shipped to you when they realized you are probably going to live a million miles away for the foreseeable future, which is hard to say out loud but, really, who are we trying to kid.

So you get all the boxes and you're like, "OMG, what is all this stuff!?"

You find your eighth-grade yearbook, your old sticker book that you and your brother co-owned in 1984 containing a mix of My Little Pony and Transformers stickers and a lot of scratch-n-sniffs that totally don't smell anymore, dozens of wallet-size prom pictures of you and someone you all but forgot about, a charm necklace, ticket stubs, Playbills, college acceptance letters, the papier-mâché puppet you made in the third grade, and letters.

Lots and lots of letters. So many letters that you start to think maybe you got hit on the head really hard and don't remember that you used to be a celebrity, because from the looks of all these stacks of letters you'd swear you had a fan club.

But as you dig through each and every letter, you see that indeed these were not fans but mainly friends and relatives, minus the unsigned letter you got in your box in high school that was creepy, weird, and threatening, which you did not know who it was from then and still don't know now so you finally throw it away, thirteen years after the fact. But other than that, it's pretty much Warm Fuzzy City. Note after handwritten note bearing sentiments like, "I miss you!" "I love you," and "I can't wait to see you again!" And some of them weren't even from your mom. There are ones that say "I am so glad we became friends." Some even comment on specific attributes: "I love your weird sense of humor!" or "You make me laugh. I will miss being roommates." You find letters from people you forgot you even liked enough to exchange letters with. You find a letter from your little sister written from summer camp circa 1992 with an urgent P.S. stating, "Tell Mom and Dad I want a trampoline for my birthday!! OK??" You're laughing as you tear through letter after letter. Except when you're reading all the ones from your late grandmother, which typically begin "My dearest, precious granddaughter…" and then you are bawling your eyes out. Which intensifies as you find the birthday card from your parents where your dad writes how glad he is that you finally moved back to Rhode Island. And then you are drowning in an ocean of homesickness and wish Boulder could just switch places with Attleboro. So you leave to go put your wash in the dryer because you can't take it anymore but when you return to the living room you see several shapeless, ill-defined stacks of letters to keep strewn about the floor, and you realize you are going to have to figure out a storage system for all these letters (which you may or may not ever look at again and, even though you know that you probably won't, find that irrelevant as there is no way you are throwing these away), but you have to leave because you have a three o'clock bike fit appointment, and you know you are going to have to come home to these amorphous piles and eventually deal with them. OK, so now you feel kind of bad and not so good anymore. But you know that whenever you have a chance to get these organized and put them in some clear stackable Sterilite containers from Target, you are definitely going to feel good again.

27

Found This Week

I'VE SAID IT before and I will say it again: Boulder streets are the Nordstrom of random free stuff. I kid you not. If you wait long enough, you will find whatever you are seeking on these streets, especially around the first of the month, when all the snot-nosed college kids who can't be bothered to take their castoffs to the Salvation Army leave them by the nearest Dumpster instead. Not that I particularly blame them. Why should they go to the extra trouble when their stuff will surely be put to good use anyway? It is not uncommon to see people, all kinds of people, ranging from those with no teeth to those such as myself who have had thousands of dollars worth of orthodontia, shopping the side streets and alleyways. On Thursday I even saw people with grocery carts and buckets with which to shuttle their new treasures.

This week I have accrued: a colander, a host of Tupperware, a wastebasket (the exact kind I actually spent money on at Bed Bath and Beyond, which is designated for the desk area; the bedroom still needed one), three wine glasses (for white wine), and a small skillet. I almost took a TV but a) It didn't have a remote and b) I don't have cable or c) DVR and if I got said TV I would feel compelled to get one of those introductory deals for both b and c and since I am using my neighbor's unsecured Internet connection for free anyway (thank you bobo, whoever you are), it doesn't really make sense, especially because d) I have pretty much been off TV ever since I moved to Boulder, save for a few presidential debates and episodes of *Family Guy* and *How I Met Your Mother* that Dan and I occasionally download on Hulu.com. Which is kind of annoying because I'm always like "Tilt the screen!" or "My head is in your armpit/collarbone/shoulder" and "WHY IS IT BUFFERING!? I WAS WATCHING THAT!" But overall this is better than an actual TV because I know from the times we have been in a hotel together that Dan and I are not compatible TV partners. And that is all I will say about that. Except that one of us really likes *SpongeBob SquarePants* and one of us doesn't. Also, one of us flips through channels as if it is somehow satisfying to see two minutes of one thousand things and one of us doesn't.

But anyway, I refuse to buy anything that either Dan has or we can register for, which is pretty much everything. I am so very looking forward to the first of the month and all the pre-owned riches it will surely bring.

28

Wishbone Waster

THE FIRST TIME, I was willing to let it go. Dan and I had roasted a chicken, and when I found the wishbone I made sure we put it up on a shelf so that it could dry out, and several months later, we each made a wish and pulled on it. He won, fair and square. After grumbling a little about my loss, I asked him what he wished for, fully expecting him to taunt me by keeping it a big secret. To my surprise (and dismay upon hearing the answer), he told me, "I wished to die in space." Die in space? What? Huh? Seriously? What does that even mean? According to Dan, it means that while some hope to die at home, in their sleep, and/or surrounded by loved ones, he wants to die on a spaceship. (Did I get that right, babe?) OK, fine. My wish would have been good for both of us, and actually could happen in this lifetime, but OK. It was his wish to make, so I let it go. And by let it go, I mean I made fun of him every chance I got, including several months later when I brought it up at the wedding of one of his college friends and everyone agreed, in between hysterical fits of laughter, that Dan had not changed a whole lot since his days as a physics major.

Just last night, on a picnic, we found ourselves with a carrot that had a very wishboney shape to it. Not one to waste an opportunity for a wish, I seized the moment and told Dan to make a wish and pull on one end. I closed my eyes and concentrated for a moment. A house in Table Mesa for under $400K (with four bedrooms and stainless appliances). One, two, three…

Dan won again!

"What'd you wish for??" I asked. Maybe he wished for a house in Table Mesa (Martin Acres would be OK too) and it would be a win-win!

"Nothing."

"Nothing!?"

"It just happened so fast!"

"Happened so fast? You could have told me to wait! You wasted a wish!!!!"

He apologized. I munched on my measly half of the carrot. I shook my head.

Dying in space was one thing, but nothing. Oh my. I am not sure which is worse.

29

The Facts Ma'am, Just the Facts

I KNOW THEY say a picture is worth a thousand words but I don't have my digital camera handy and the world NEEDS TO KNOW ABOUT THIS RIGHT NOW so words will have to suffice. Anyway this not a photo gallery.

So here's the deal. Everything is normal circa thirty minutes ago. Dan and I were at his place working from home. I know it sounds like maybe we weren't really working (or am I just projecting my insecurities and fears here?) and, really, I can't speak for Dan, but I was definitely interspersing work and work-related emails with Facebook and compulsive blog reading. I was at the dining room table. Dan was in his room. (Right. We don't live together. And don't try to tell me there is no way I can know if I should marry him without living with him first because I will just smile and nod to your face and then behind your back I will say to the first person I see "WTF!? Since when is [your name here] such a relationship *fucking expert!?* Because [your name here] can just go fuck him/herself because, guess what, I never asked whether I should live with Dan before we get married, OK!? When I want relationship advice, I WILL ASK FOR IT!!!" And then I will have to take a Valium. OK, just kidding about the Valium; I will not take one, but I will want one.

OK, so I digressed there. The point is that earlier in the day, Dan had asked me if I would like for him to get me a coffee. But I politely declined because then I would have had to wake up and drink it, and I didn't want to do it right then. It was early. OK, it was 8:00 but guess what, people—when you work from home, yes, you can do it in your pjs, but it also means sometimes you stay up till, like, midnight working. Like last night, I was working till 11:15. Not that I need to justify myself, I'm just…turning into my mother, the original not-a-morning person… OK that is a whole other story… But anyway, when I finally woke up and started working, of course I was thinking about coffee and how much I wanted some. Being that my coffee pot is at my house and I wasn't going there, the equidistant coffee shop was the only option. So everything was good in my world because a) I was about to get coffee and b) Dan was actually going to bring his laptop to the coffee shop with me so we could work (or blog as the case may be) together. Yay!!

So he gave me the five-minute warning, at which point I shut down my computer and donned my shoes. As I put my laptop in my bag, I glanced at Dan out of the corner of my eye and did a double take. Why was he wearing his Halloween costume from last year when we dressed up as a schoolgirl (me) and a dirty old man (him)? It wasn't like he had candy and beer in his coat pockets like he did on Halloween, but it was basically the same exact outfit; he had on a heather gray T-shirt with some weird math equation on it. (No, I am not kidding. Seriously, could I even make that up?) The collar was frayed and there was a pea-size hole in the back, right under his left shoulder blade. The edges of the sleeves were fraying too. His shorts were of the cargo variety, and their light khaki shade almost matched his T-shirt exactly. I will give him credit for his low-rise Adidas socks (because he prefers the same tube socks he has had for, like, ten years) and his new Asics sneakers. Over his outfit (I use the term "outfit" loosely) he had on his black knee length pea coat. As I started to form the words to say something in protest to this ensemble, he took his famous homeless person/tuque type hat out of his pocket.

"Dan, you can't wear that outfit."

"Why not?"

"You either need to change your coat or put on jeans. That outfit is not OK."

"But it's not like I'm single. Who cares what I wear?"

"But I have to be seen with you. Like, hey, everyone, my fiancé is homeless." Which is actually funny because a long time ago I dated someone who didn't really have anywhere to live, and for some reason, like when you're reading a fiction book, I was able to engage that phenomenon, Suspension of Disbelief. And for some reason, here, now, I was not able to do that with Dan. Maybe because I am older now, more mature…

But anyway, I really wanted to go for coffee, so we walked to the coffee shop even though he was wearing that stupid outfit. I told him he was a walking fashion faux pas and he was like, "You should totally blog about this!" and I was like, "Would you mind if I make fun of you on my blog?" And he said, "Sure. As long as you include all the facts."

30

The Case of the Missing iPod

I USED TO be a major impulse buyer. I am not saying I'm not still prone to going to SierraTradingPost.com for one thing, like a new bathing suit since my old one is on the verge of losing its elastic, and then filling up my cart with other things since I am already ordering something anyway, things in various sizes and colors, since I might as well return five things if I am going to return one anyway, and next thing I know I have, like, four hundred dollars worth of merchandise in my cart, including cycling attire for Dan, which he won't even appreciate but I will. So, yeah, I admit I do that sometimes, maybe I even did it this week, but for the most part, I have really learned to rein myself in over the past eighteen months or so, which was concurrent with the time that I a) no longer had a full-time job; b) no longer had paid leave or any portion of paid health benefits; c) very nearly ran out of money; and d) decided it was time to start saving for a house. So I e) got my act together and realized that, by and large, even though there are things I want, I will not explode if I don't get them into my possession RIGHT NOW.

That being said, for a few months I had been eying the iTrip. This handy device lets you tune into a radio frequency and then plug your iPod into the cigarette lighter and voila—you are listening to your iPod in the car. It's like magic. I really wanted one, especially because my car CD player has been malfunctioning for, like, the last four years, and I have not been able to bring myself to pay someone to fix it. Even though I wanted the iTrip really bad as early as Septemberish, I made an executive decision to delay gratification and therefore chose to purchase the iTrip as my birthday present from me to me in November.

So on the day of my thirty-first birthday (which was a glorious day including indulgences such as opening a present in bed, going out to breakfast, Dan not only agreeing to but suggesting that we enter Target together, a massage, a swim in the heated outdoor lap pool, and a cake called Better than Sex, which was only a little disturbing since it was baked by my future mother-in-law but the fact that it was chocolately goodness in its ultimate form more than compensated for any possible awkwardness that may have arisen from this cake's unseemly name), I went to the Apple Store and bought my iTrip.

It was the perfect companion for what would be my nearly two-hour commute to work the following day. For reasons that pertain largely to my ineptitude and generosity, I had agreed to help out where I was apparently desperately needed in Greeley (see the latter), but then got way lost and my seventy-five-minute trip became much longer (see the former). I arrived at the facility finally. Unsure of where to park, I helped myself to a space in visitor parking, which I kind of was, what with being per diem and all, knowing the chances of my "visiting" again were quite slim given the distance of this place from my home. The area looked decidedly sketchy so I decided to keep my iPod in my jacket pocket instead of in my car. We all know what can happen when we accidentally leave prized electronic possessions in the car.

As I got out of the car, I was struck by how horrid the long-term-care facility smelled, noting that not all nursing homes were created equal, and then remembered that that's just how the air smells in Greeley. Although the odor seems like the smell of an old person who has soiled themselves and been ignored, especially when you are standing by a huge nursing home, it's actually the drift of the manure-scented air of the rural northern Colorado town that you're smelling.

Work was fairly busy and went by fast. Around 4:30, I reached for my lavender Patagonia that had been hanging on the coat tree in the therapy office. I slunk into my jacket and felt in my pockets and was immediately alarmed by the emptiness I felt. The iPod was not there. I checked again, frantically. I looked in my purse and in my lunch bag just in case, as my stomach dropped with the knowledge that someone had stolen my iPod. I knew it was supposed to be in my jacket pocket because for a brief second during my lunch break, I had given my jacket pocket a quick feel, just to make sure it was still there. I know what I felt and it was my iPod. I was especially sure of it because I had stupidly left my phone at home, so it could not have been my phone that I felt. My iPod was there at lunch and now it wasn't. Why why why did I decide not to wear my coat to the home evaluation that lasted forever? I'm not saying it wasn't worth every last one of the 120 or so minutes I spent there, it's just that when you have a 1950s ranch home that has never been renovated and a rotund, debilitated gentleman who will be going back to said home on two liters of oxygen at all times, some issues arise and that means if you are his occupational therapist assessing said home situation for safety, you have to take some extra time to explain some things, like why said gentleman's ninety-pound wife should NOT EVER walk down the rickety rail-less basement stairs in front of him in order to break his possible fall because actually he would crush her if he were to fall and what they really need are a) railings on the stairs down to the basement, or better yet b) a shower on the main level that he can actually access, but since b is not possible refer back to a. If you can address this problem and others like it in an hour or less, tell me how and I will give you a free iPod.

Anyway, I felt certain that my iPod had been ripped from my possession during that home visit when I was miles from my jacket, which I actually wished I had because it was colder than I thought it would be. I approached the other therapists who happened to be finishing up their paperwork in the office. There was a neon sign in my brain flashing "SOMEONE HERE STOLE MY IPOD!!!!" I said calmly, "Has anyone seen an iPod? I can't find mine." Someone suggested perhaps I left it in my car. But I knew this was not possible, as I remembered specifically placing it in my jacket pocket and feeling for it at lunch. One of the physical therapists vouched for me, stating how I specifically mentioned to her that I brought the iPod into work instead of leaving it in my car when we were talking earlier that day about the questionable neighborhood and the parking situation. I got sympathetic glances, surprise, and concern that a thief might be in the building, and a couple people peered around on the floor looking for the iPod but none of this was enough to bring my device back.

I drove home facing the sun as it set quickly behind the purple-tinted mountains and felt bad for myself, as much as for having my iPod stolen as for getting lost again on the way home, not once but twice. Yes, I know it's a no-brainer that when you're going west you should be facing the mountains, but I thought maybe it was just foggier than I thought and was so mad at myself when I finally noticed them. In my rearview mirror. At which point I took the first possible opportunity for a U-turn. My long drive was now even longer, without even the company of my favorite playlists or the GPS that was ruthlessly stolen from me almost exactly a year ago. I couldn't even call Dan and whine about it because I forgot my phone. I whined to myself for most of the drive home instead. When I told Dan, he felt bad for me, but I still didn't feel better. My mom called me the next morning, but I just couldn't get excited about her meeting with the wedding florist, partly due to the fact that flowers are flowers as far as I am concerned, except pink peonies, which I really love and hope to have in my bouquet, but beyond that what else is there to talk about, and partly because I was just bummed about the missing iPod. Why had I even bothered going to work? It would cost me as much as I earned that day just to buy a new one. Or could I live without one? Probably. But why should I be having to debate whether I should live without one or not? The point was, I was violated. It felt icky to know that someone I probably worked with reached into my pocket and took my property. Were they bopping to my "Wake Up" playlist right now? Were they relaxing with my "What the who-ha" (don't ask) playlist? Did they trade it for crystal meth? I would never know.

The next day I worked at a different building, glad to be going to a place where I was more of a regular, a facility right down the street from me that happens to be an affiliate of the iPod-stealing, manure-smelling, seventy-miles-away-but-ninety-if-you-get-lost Greeley facility. Within a couple of hours, one of the managers from said facility called me to say how sorry she was that my iPod had apparently been stolen on their property. I appreciated her call but still felt disheartened. When my manager arrived at work, I asked for five minutes of his time and explained the case of the missing iPod. He felt bad and said he would email the regional manager to alert him of the problem.

The next day was Saturday, and I was scheduled to work, this time at the hospital. After pressing snooze for the millionth time,

I donned my scrubs and tried to not feel bad for myself for working on a weekend. It shouldn't matter, considering I end up not working a lot of weekdays, but there is always a lingering feeling of "I shouldn't be working today" when I work on a weekend. Anyway, like usual, the sun was shining and this bolstered my mood somewhat. Headed west, I was thinking about stopping at Vic's for an Americano and pondered whether there was actually time to get my fix and arrive at work on time (there was) when I spotted something black and shiny out of the corner of my eye. It looked suspiciously like an iPod. My iPod to be exact. But how could this be? Did someone perhaps feel badly and return it? But did they really drive all the way from Greeley just to somehow insert the iPod in my car without breaking any windows or anything? It seemed impossible. Perhaps it was just some random iPod…that randomly inserted itself in my car? At the next red light, I checked the playlist menu and, sure enough, all my playlists were there. So it was definitely my iPod. I was overwhelmed with shame. Not only had I made news of the stolen iPod public around work, I had even posted it on Facebook. What kind of tool thinks their iPod was stolen when it was in their car the whole time??? The same kind of person who is sure their landlord must have come in and stole their broom when actually it was kind of hard to see the broom behind the door and it was therefore inexplicably missing for a couple weeks. In other words, me. After I called both of my managers and explained my blunder, the cloud of embarrassment lifted somewhat. I guess the moral of this story is even if you think you know something, like for instance you are 100 percent sure your iPod was in your pocket, it is still possible that you don't know anything at all and you better really check your facts before you go around feeling violated and telling everyone about it.

31

The End of an Era

THINGS ARE CHANGING, and fast. Ever since Wednesday, my world has been flipped upside down. Wednesday was the fateful day on which I had my first appointment with a nutrition counselor at my gym. I had been curious for a long time about what a nutrition consult could do for me. The one conclusion I typically came to after pondering this question was: It would mean less money in my pocket and a potentially dreadfully boring, bland diet. This did not entice me in the least.

Until I ran into a friend at our tri club Halloween party. He said that if he had only a finite amount of money to spend on triathlon (Wait, what? We don't all have unlimited funds for Ironmans, 70.3 races, associated travel and lodging, a new wetsuit, the latest greatest tri bike, and of course the fastest lightest wheels, and all the requisite healthy groceries, a coach, a gym membership, and all the Hammer products you need to keep you satiated and hydrated??) that he would spend it on a nutritionist versus a coach because his nutritionist helped him TONS. I wanted to know more. He told me he was actually supposed to eat MORE after meeting with his nutritionist and he lost tons of body fat and improved his performance drastically. I thought about this for a while. Then I thought about how I want to commit this season to having the best performance possible. And, yeah, I admit it, I thought about the fact that more than a hundred people are going to be looking at me all at the same time when I get married this summer, and if that doesn't make a woman want to look as good as possible, then I don't know what does. And if that makes me vain, I can't help it; I get it from my dad.

So Wednesday was the fateful day. Over the phone, Seriously Fit and Healthy (a.k.a. my nutrition counselor, henceforth known as SFH) told me she did not believe in crash diets, quick fixes, weird ingredients, or fads. OK, I could get behind that. She was into small changes. I'm down with that. Her fee was about what I expected (a lot), but I was ready to commit. I arrived at our scheduled appointment with the food journal I had been diligently keeping all week per SFH's request. I know I eat a lot of bites of this and nibbles of that and always have, but it was a real eye-opener to put it all down on paper. I neither stopped nibbling nor neglected to record it, for how could SFH help me if she did not know what kind of nibble addict she was dealing with?

She went through my food journal with a critical eye, crossing out things she did not like (one lemon cookie, a bite of Dan's raspberry scone, most of half a pastrami sandwich even though was not hungry plus about ten fries and several bites of coleslaw), and starred some of the things she liked (quinoa with veggie and tofu stir-fry, salad, low-fat cottage cheese and light peaches), and then she looked at me with her big, seriously fit brown eyes and said, "It's not that bad. For now, I just want to make a couple of changes. Small changes. But I want you to commit to them and really, really do them." I nodded. I was ready. She went on.

"First, I want you to get in the habit of measuring out your half-and-half so you know how much one tablespoon is and only put that much in your coffee."

I nodded. I can do that. I might end up thinking I might as well drink it black, but I can do that. I nodded again, as if daring her to give me another challenge.

"Also, you need to stop nibbling."

As obvious as it was, I needed to pay someone to tell me to do that. I figure I eat, like, 100 to 300 empty calories on any given day with all the random bites I take of random stuff, but I needed professional help to take on this challenge. I nodded again. I was ready to breathe a sigh of relief. I had received my mission: Two small changes to commit to. I was ready. And then she continued.

"And also, this is going to be kind of a challenge [actually in Boulder it really is only kind of a challenge because every other person you meet is gluten-free/dairy-free/sugar-free, etc.] but I want you to try giving up gluten." She went on to describe all the great health benefits I may experience with this (more energy, fewer stomachaches, less bloating, less gas, lean out the midsection, what was she saying about my midsection anyway?) and how I should try it and see if it helps. I was ready to get pouty and whine, "But you said two! That's THREE!" but I kept my mouth shut for once and just nodded. If that's what she wanted, I would do it. Except I did tell her I was having girls night that night and chances were high that gluten would be involved, as I was not hosting. SFH found some mercy in her seriously fit heart and said I could start tomorrow.

Thursday was uneventful, as I brought my lunch to work. I was offered a small slice of cheesecake but knew the crust had gluten and feared the slice was too small to be considered a dessert and rather was a nibble, so I politely declined. Thursday evening brought trivia at the D Note, where I was sure I would be relegated to a choice of salad or salad but was delighted to find gluten-free pizza crust on the menu. It was gross but it was gluten-free. Poor Dan got to be gluten-free too. Friday was, again, uneventful save for the tri club Christmas party, where I accepted a passed hors d'oeurve of bread with some olive tapenade before I even knew what I was doing. Oopsies. I did, however, avoid all other possible threats like the lasagna and the pulled-pork slider, and, oh, the chicken quesadilla, which looked so cheesy, salty, and all-around good. Saturday, when we were over at friends' for dinner, I ate the pecan pie but not the crust, which was surprisingly not that hard to do. I would like to say this is temporary and, like SFH said, we can try it and if it doesn't help anything, I can stop, but I am going to have be quite honest. It feels good not to eat bread and stuff. Good enough to do forever, I am not sure. Good enough to do while my money goes in SFH's bank account? Definitely. Good-bye unlimited half-and-half, nibbles, and gluten. It was good while it lasted. And I know we will meet again, if only at birthdays and weddings.

32

Creepy McCreeperson (a.k.a. Creep Depot)

OK, SO EVERYTHING was going good. Dan and I started our house hunt and after seeing, like, eight properties I was like, "OK, not only am I more of a princess than I even thought I was, but we are never going to find anything because of said princess problem!" Everything we saw seemed wrong somehow. The bi-level seemed somehow weird. The three-bedroom homes just…didn't have enough bedrooms. There was one awesome one except you had to turn sideways to enter the kitchen. There was another great house, but only if you planned on having zero to a maximum of one child, who would remain an infant/toddler indefinitely. Then we saw a bi-level that I thought I could learn to love, and Dan was like, "But you don't like bi-levels!" The realtor said I was allowed to change my mind while I made a "No doy" face at Dan. I wanted to like one that was a little bigger than the others, but you could hear the traffic from Foothills Parkway in the front yard, which was not cool.

But then we saw the ninth property and it was like love at first sight! Hardwood floors! Remodeled kitchen with granite counters! A remodeled bathroom! Plenty of space! A totally finished basement! A brand-new fence! The real estate gods smiled upon us and our offer was accepted. The realtor sent us a series of emails regarding the many tasks we must complete prior to the closing. The list grew increasingly longer and I realized that while I have put my name next to more than 95 percent of the tasks on our wedding to do list, a) our housing was possibly more important than our wedding day (I said possibly, people) and b) even though I am starting to understand interest rates and points, Dan is SO much better at that stuff and therefore better equipped to handle it, but even so c) I had to take a couple of things off Dan's plate so d) instead of calling the inspector or the mortgage loan people I would e) volunteer to look up neighborhood crime stats and collect info on any registered sex offenders in my neighborhood and btw I am now f) totally freaked out that someone will google sex offenders and find me.

But anyway, I started to look up sex offenders and it was CREEPY. I mean creepier than running-before-dawn-near-the-creek creepy. Creepier than that weird guy I used to work with who was, like, my dad's age and constantly saying the most inappropriate things—to me and all the other girls too. And rubbing up against us in inappropriate ways, and intermittently saying lewd things to our supervisor during team meetings. (No, I did not make that up. I could not make that up if I tried. I wish it was not true.) Creepier than having a patient in the hospital who had a boner for, like, our entire occupational therapy session (which I later found out was just a penile implant, after all. Was I disappointed? Maybe a little. IS THERE A LAW AGAINST BEING CREEPED OUT AND SIMULTANEOUSLY FLATTERED? Didn't think so.)

So anyway, this list is gross. Like I was saying, every face on there I was like, "Did I see him in King Soopers last week?" "Was that the guy I thought was looking at me funny when I was running this morning at dawn?" "OMG, that guy's address IS ON THE SAME BLOCK AS WHERE I USED TO LIVE" Ew ew ew ew ew ew. I couldn't look at the whole list at once. But I will do it. I will do it because it means I get to check "Look up sex offenders" off my to-do list, which means there will (hopefully) be one less thing to delay or prevent our closing, which means I will finally have what I always wanted, which is to share a home with the man of my dreams!!! Which is saccharine but true. And while it may be gross, it is NOT creepy.

33

Agnostic Maybe Starting to Think There Could Be a God

LAST NIGHT WHEN I was driving home from a friend's in Denver, my driver-side window started acting funny. I noticed it was cracked open, which was weird because it was a) freezing out, and b) I didn't remember touching it. But anyway, I hit the window up button and nothing happened. Maybe the window was frozen to the door or something? I kept driving, intermittently trying to get my window to go up when suddenly I heard *kerplunk*. That is the sound of a 2003 Jetta driver-side window falling akimbo into the door. What does "falling akimbo" mean, you might be wondering? It means the window kind of flipped on its side and fell in so that the corner was facing up... Kind of like when your sliding closet door goes off track, only you are driving on I-25 at night in the dead of winter with cold air blowing in your face, and you still have thirty-five minutes, at least, till you get home. You have the heat blasting, your wool hat on, and your hood up, but you are freezing and terrified so you decide not to try and mess with the window any more, lest it shatter into a million pieces into your freezing lap, and you really want to get home tonight.

This morning I called Safelite AutoGlass. Luckily, they could come to my work and fix it onsite. Not so luckily, they couldn't get out till tomorrow. That left me with two choices for today: drive to work and leave my car with the window wide open in a public parking lot, or drive Dan's car to work. After much deliberation, I chose the latter. The problem with Dan's car is that it has a standard transmission. My experience with driving his car thus far included a lot of cursing, holding my breath, and yelling "What fucking gear am I in!? WHAT GEAR!? WHERE IS THIRD?" That was my role anyway. Dan's role was to gently coach me, to encourage me, and to kindly inform me of what gear I was in. I wasn't sure what I would do without him on my first solo mission.

I decided to go for a little test drive. I took the car around the block and even made a three-point turn when I got to a dead end. "I think I can do this!" I told myself. Positive self-talk is key. I got to the end of our street and put my blinker on to turn left onto the main road. As soon as I saw someone in my rearview, I thought better of my decision and put on my hazards instead. She kindly pulled up next to me, rolled down her window, and asked if I was OK. I thanked her and said I was just learning to drive the car. For the first time in my life, I hoped that she would think I was sixteen and just learning to drive, period, as I felt that would knock down the embarrassment factor a few notches. As it turned out, my first victory was imminent, as I successfully turned left up a slight hill. OK, just twenty-five more miles to go… I could do this. I left my hazards on just in case. Then as I approached each red light, I crawled as slow as I could and gave dirty looks in my rearview mirror to any vehicle that dared come within twenty feet of my car, lest I have to stop and start again, a.k.a. recipe for disaster, as I really had to be at work and did not budget time for stalling. Nor had I even come close to finishing my coffee.

As I continued cruising south on Highway 93, I started to feel pretty confident. Not confident enough to turn off my hazards, mind you, but OK to mess with the radio. But it was set to some fuzzy AM station, and I was going to have to mess with my drink holder to find KBCO, and all of a sudden I got really nervous and turned the radio right off. But even so, I was doing OK. But, just in case, I prayed that anyone behind me would note my hazard lights and stay very far back because otherwise I might have a total panic attack.

And then the inevitable happened. I stalled at the intersection of U.S. 6 and Colfax. It was a proverbial red light on a hill, and I had no choice but to stop. When I tried to go again, I killed the engine. So I tried again. And again. And again. And again. And again. And again. I lost count of how many light cycles I missed after about four. Because it was just so dang many or because my thoughts turned from "You can do this. Relax. Visualize the car going. OK, try it another way. OK, more gas. Less clutch. Less gas. More cowbell" to…stuff I can't write down, I don't know. Remember the "Everybody Hurts" video by REM and how all the people are really sad in their individual cars? Imagine a video of one adult throwing a tantrum in the car yelling very uncouth things so loudly and so repetitively that it made her throat hurt, which it still does a little, more than twelve hours later, and imagine the song is called "This Person Is Totally Losing Her Shit."

My state evolved from totally melting down to relieved and too out of control to even be embarrassed when a state trooper in an SUV pulled up behind me with his flashers on. He had a beard. I always imagined if there was a god, he would have a beard. Well, my god has a long white beard, but this guy's auburn beard would do just fine. In any case, if he wasn't god, he was an angel sent from god. Did I mention I am an agnostic who is starting to believe there may be a god? Anyway, he comes up to my car and he's like, "Are you OK?" or something, and I am crying like a baby and in between sobs I'm like, "This isn't my car. My car window is busted. This is my fiancé's car. And I can't make it go." So he's like, "OK, take a deep breath." Then he reminded me it's Tuesday, not Monday, therefore not that bad, which made me smile a little. He told me to put the car in gear. I wiped my eyes and said, "It is," and then he said, "It's in neutral." And then I yanked on the thing and sure enough it was in neutral. And then I got into first and I made it to work with no other problems, except stalling on the way into the parking lot and arriving two minutes late, which no one seemed to mind.

On the way home, I got a little cocky and even ate a banana while driving. I was quickly humbled when my car stalled again, this time in major rush-hour traffic. A handsome-looking guy approached my car. I admit it was kind of him to risk his safety by pulling over and crossing two or three busy lanes of traffic to try and help me, but unless you're a policeman, if you're a man I don't know, I am not inviting you into my car. Or Dan's car, as the case may be. Maybe I have read a few too many Ann Rule books, but I'm just sayin'. So anyway, this guy asks me if I would like to have him help me get my car to the breakdown lane, so at least no one will rear-end me. I said, "No, thank you." He said, "Are you sure? You could get rear-ended." I said, "I know, but I don't think that will happen." Then confidently I added, "Seriously, this has happened to me before. I'll be OK." Take that, helpful hot guy! Did I mention he was hot? He was hot. Still, I knew I could do it. And I did, eventually. All the way till I got halfway into our driveway, then I tried to reverse so I could park on the street, but the car stalled again and I had run out of patience, and I left the car there, ran into the house, and asked Dan to please come out and park it for me because I was done. But even so, I did it, I lived, I think maybe there's a god now, and also I need to tell my brother I win, because when we were kids we used to try and see who could best impersonate our dad when the press broke at his scrap metal yard and he would have his moment of special rage reserved only for the press breaking, and I think I nailed it, although I was not trying to impersonate anyone.

34

Thank You for the Lovely Fire Extinguisher(s)

LAST NIGHT WE had a housewarming party. Sorry if you are reading this and weren't invited; it's probably because I hate you, as we invited virtually everyone we know. Just kidding. If I know you and didn't invite you it's probably only because I forgot or didn't have your email address. Anyway, it was a very successful potluck. What makes a party successful, you ask? Lots of things, among them, the PDDF (Pam Dessert Degeneration Factor), or how quickly did I go from "not going to eat any desserts because my wedding is in about two months" to "just going to try that one that looks really good, anyway two months is actually kind of a long time" to "OMG, I don't hardly have room for that eighth dessert…which means, yes, of course, I have a little room for that banana cream pie…did someone say chocolate ice cream? Wedding? What wedding??"

When the pesto pasta, pot stickers, pudding cakes, and pinot noir were put away, the last crumbs swept up, and the empty bottles collected in the recycle bin, we went through the presents.

There were the usual suspects: bottles of wine, especially nice bottles of wine, scented candles… And then we opened a tissue paper–covered rectangle, which revealed…a fire extinguisher. And then we opened a gift bag full of tea accoutrements, and then I remembered the neon green gift bag I left in the basement. Which contained none other than…a second fire extinguisher. Two fire extinguishers? Is that a little weird? It's what I would have expected of my brother, but our friends? Do they know how accident-prone I am? Is that what this is about? Is this a normal thing for someone to give to another adult who is neither their sibling nor their offspring? (Our third fire extinguisher was a gift to Dan from his parents when he bought his condo years ago.) Three fire extinguishers!? Is it me or is this excessive? Yesterday, Dan asked me just how many serving platters we need and if we can start to pare down once we have "enough." Whatever that means. I looked at him blankly. (I mean, hello, the bamboo serving tray is perfect for breakfast in bed and/or shuttling food out to the patio, once we have some patio furniture. Or for our as yet unborn children to take their Eggo waffles and pizza bagels down to the basement, where they can watch their allotted daily hour of TV on the television we don't yet have… And the red serving tray is festive and meant for appetizers at parties, while the white one is better for chicken, turkey, or prime rib on holidays, and the white one with the blue flowers is more of a dessert tray, I think.) So anyway, I get what Dan means about paring down. When it comes to fire extinguishers, not necessarily other stuff.

35

I Get Lost and Dan Bails Me Out: Part Who-Even-Can-Count-That-High

THIS WEEKEND WE were in Los Angeles for a friend's wedding. I was looking forward to my Saturday run, as I think running in a new place is a fantastic way to explore it. I was also well aware that my sense of direction is abominable and am actually beginning to wonder if maybe some crucial brain development ceased when my brother threw the eight ball at my head from the top of the steps when we were kids. The eight ball was confiscated and my brother was punished and that made me feel good, but I will never get my sense of direction back, and that frustrates me, but luckily with modern technology you barely need a sense of direction these days anyway. Although it would help a lot, which I learned for, like, the millionth time this weekend.

So I laced up my shoes and strapped on my Garmin (which was, in fact, a gift from said brother, actually mostly because he was worried about me and he thought the navigation function might help, and come to think of it was this gift maybe his subtle way of apologizing for the whole eight ball thing?? I haven't told him this but now I guess I am telling the whole world, so, Adam, if you are reading this you might as well know, I don't even know how to use the navigation function. I use the Garmin for pace, distance, heart rate, and lap splits, and it is one of the best gifts I have ever received, even though I don't use it for its intended function). While I was getting ready to go, I went over my route once again with our gracious host, who was trying to tell me how to get to the reservoir. It was, like, up the stairs, left at the cactus, right at the supermodern house, then down for a while and around. "That sounds pretty straightforward. I got it." Dan looked skeptical. I insisted I understood the directions and I would be FINE. I felt like a drunk probably feels when he swears he can have ONE beer. Dan insisted I take my iPhone. If I didn't love that damn phone so much I probably would have succumbed to my inner child and asserted my FINEness once more, just to be defiant, but instead I agreed it probably wouldn't hurt to have the mapping software (just in case, because, like I said, I was FINE).

So with my phone in hand, I stepped out into the glorious oxygen-(and smog-)filled sea-level air and started my journey. And oh my god did it feel good. When I come down to sea level, I realize just how much training at altitude makes me feel like I am breathing through a straw. This was pure heaven. I could breathe! I COULD BREATHE! Big, deep, decadent, luxurious breaths of oxygen-rich AIR. With green stuff all around! Trees, leaves, bushes, stems, cacti, it was all gloriously green! I'd forgotten how much my eyes love the sight of green. When I wasn't enjoying the green lushness of the landscape, I was admittedly staring at my phone, trying to figure out where I was and how to get to the reservoir. It was like they were trying to hide it or something, it was so tricky to find, but with the help of Google Maps I made it to the reservoir and there I was able to run without the nuisance of worrying about where I was. All I had to do was keep the water on my left. Which I did, except when I messed up at one point and ended up, well, somewhere, I don't know where, really, but I eventually made it back to the reservoir. I was so happy! My legs felt light and free, and with all this air I was able to run FAST! According to my Garmin, I was running a 7:30 to 8:15 pace and I wasn't even out of zone 1. I was fantasizing about moving to L.A. and running fast every day when I completed my second loop around the reservoir and decided this was getting old and the best thing to do would be to check out different parts of the neighborhood. The only way to go was up. And it just kept going…up and up and up and up. When I finally crested the hill, I paused to enjoy the view.

Then I went down for a while and around. I looked at my watch. I meant to run for about an hour and I was at the forty-five-minute mark so I consulted my phone. My battery was getting low, so I was trying to be conservative about my phone use (and picture taking, but it was just so pretty I couldn't help taking a few), but I had no idea where I was. Luckily, Google Maps knew exactly where I was. I mapped out some directions to get me back and I resumed the run. Everything was going well until I got to a place where there was supposed to be a road, but there was just someone's fenced yard. A nice dog-walking man approached me to see if I needed any help. I told him where I was trying to go and he told me how to get there. I remember him saying something about left and down but as I headed left, the only way to go was up and up some more. I felt confident that I was getting closer when Dan called. I was totally in the zone, charging up this hill while my battery was slowly dying, so I kept it brief. In between panting for breath I told him I was fine and I would be back soon, and the map was great, not to worry. Until a few blocks later, when I realized I was actually getting farther from where I wanted to be, and actually I need to own up to something here. I don't just have a bad sense of direction. I also have a really hard time reading maps. It has gotten better over time, especially within the past five years, which is about the time I actually started learning how to read them (my prior rationale being, why use a map when you can just get a cue sheet? Who needs a map when you live in a place like Rhode Island where there are no street signs and all the landmarks are stuff that used to be there twenty-plus years ago, e.g., Go left where Sears used to be). So anyways, yes, I have made it my business to read maps more, and I actually like looking at maps to learn a new place, but it remains an area for personal development. I was getting really confused and frustrated. I was thirsty and I didn't feel like running all morning. I had to pace myself. There was a wedding later on, and I was not about to bonk before the main event. And did I mention there were hills?

Running around here made me realize why that show I may or may not really enjoy that takes place in the Los Angeles valley is called *The Hills*. It's not that I'm a quitter. I mean, I have done two Ironmans and not fast. Quitters don't do that. It's that I am (at times) a realist. The facts were:

> I was lost.
> Every road was supercurvy so nothing made sense.
> I didn't feel like doing any more hills just to realize I went the wrong way.
> My phone was dying and I was afraid I would miss my window to call Dan to come get me.
> I didn't want to miss what promised to be an amazing brunch.
> I still had not had any coffee and I knew there was some back at the house.

So I called Dan and told him what corner I was at. I heard Dan repeat it to our host as they pulled up Google Maps and heard our host say, "She's all the way over there?" While I waited for Dan, I stretched and watched all the hot little sports cars go by. Every car that wasn't a sports car gave me hope that it could be Dan, as I had no idea from what direction he would be coming, and I had pretty much forgotten everything about our rental car except that it was silver and not a convertible or a minivan.

Finally, he came for me. I bounced into the car and we giggled about how I always end up in this situation and he always bails me out and thank god for him, etc. But seriously, thank god for him. I always wanted to marry someone who was smart, kind, funny, and patient, but I forgot to add to my checklist "needs to be able to put up with me and my sense of direction." Thank you, universe for taking care of that for me by sending me Dan.

36

The Blogs Are Scaring Me

LATELY, PEOPLE HAVE been asking me and Dan if we plan to start a family. Who are "people"? Just…people. Like the guy who knocked on our door the other day and promised he wasn't selling anything just that he had lived here years ago and he was curious what new renovations had been done since he moved out in the early nineties and could he have a peek. During the grand tour, he also happened to tell us how much he paid for the house in 1985 and how much he sold it for in 1995, and then I went in the bathroom and cried. OK, not really, but I wanted to. Or our next-door neighbor. We dropped over a couple of weeks ago to invite him to our housewarming party and introduce ourselves. (No, the neighbors did not come in droves bearing homemade cookies and casseroles the day they saw our moving truck. Not a one. We did have one neighbor come over the day after we moved in partly to welcome us to the neighborhood but mostly to let us know our floodlight shines directly into his bedroom window and could we please turn it off at night.) So anyhow, we're standing on our neighbor's front stoop, and he's like, "Do you have any kids?" and

Dan cheerfully (as always) said, "Not yet!" while I turned white and shook my head. As the story goes—the story being the one said neighbor told (repeatedly, from what I heard) at our party, laughing—"One of them said, 'Not yet!' enthusiastically and the other one gave him a dirty look."

Well, let me just clear a few things up. One of them is worried about peak oil, a possible water shortage in the Southwest, and the stock market; prefers to watch stuff like *The Daily Show*; and reads financial blogs with names like Calculated Risk. The other one is worried about what heart rate she is supposed to be training in and whether she can press snooze one more time and still make it to work on time even if the coffee maker messes up again and she has to hit Vic's on the way; prefers to watch stuff like *If I Can Dream* and *The Bachelor*; and reads mostly triathlon blogs and a few mom blogs. When and if a pregnancy occurs, one will be trying to stay out of the way of some nasty moods and demanding requests (not really an adjustment) and the other one will be bloated and hormonal (more than normal).

And another thing. Imagine if you watched Fox News all day long. Wouldn't you be scared? After a while you might be terrified of national healthcare and social programs and a black president... No, never mind—that is a really bad analogy because Fox doesn't broadcast actual news and I think the anchors are fake. They all look like Stepford Wives to me, except the men, who look kind of like Ken dolls. And they are trying to scare you; that is their whole point. And just for the record, don't get the wrong idea, I don't actually watch Fox News. I don't even have a TV, remember? I just catch bits of it here and there, sometimes at the gym and usually in patients' hospital rooms. So, no, let me try again here... Reading these mom blogs...and the triathlon blogs too, considering many of the authors are moms—those scare the BEJEEZUS out of me. I read Ann Rule before bed, so it's not like any stupid thing will scare me. I know it's not about me, but when I read these blogs that are like, "I feel guilty not being with my kid because I am training/I couldn't work out because my kid vomited/My peers think I am a bad mom because I train a lot/People are telling me the baby will fall right out if I run during pregnancy," I want to comment, "Please stop scaring me!!!!" But I leave the comment field blank because obviously they have enough to worry about without being concerned or, more likely, annoyed that some grown woman finds their blog scary. And then there's the other type of blog that I try to avoid, but like a lot of my favorite blogs and TV shows, they have that train-wreck-like quality about them that makes you not be able to help but stop and stare, those ones that are like, "My child is the best thing ever/My child is the most beautiful perfect creature in the world/I did not understand love until this person came into my life"—those are like Kirsten Dunst times a thousand. In other words, gag me with a spoon. P.S. I hate Kirsten Dunst. I think she is plain looking and mildly attractive at best and has no talent for acting, and when I see her in a movie it makes me mad that I can't have her part.

And that's just the blogs. Actual people are just as scary, if not more so. I was on a plane once and I heard this lady in the row in front of me telling her seat mate, "Having a child is like having your heart beating outside your chest." Gee, where can I sign up? Or one of my patients in the hospital today, who told me, "Having kids flips your life upside down. You can't just wait to do laundry when you are down to your last pair of underwear when you have kids." I wanted to ask her why not, but I didn't. A few years ago I was having dinner at a friend's house. We sat down with her husband and two wee ones (one of whom was having some kind of conniption fit about not wanting to eat his dinner), and I asked my friend, "Hey do you ever feel like—" and she interrupted me to say, "Like slitting my wrists? Yes. All the time." (If I remember correctly, the wee one ate four bites of dinner and then he got an ice cream, and my friend's wrists remain intact.)

I am not saying I don't like kids. I mean, I was one. Kids are great. Some are exceptionally cute, especially my niece. The children are our future. I am just saying I'm scared of having them and no one seems to care, especially the Internet. I know the best thing I could do for myself if I do intend to someday have a family is lay off the blogs. But seriously. There is work to be procrastinated and lots of it. I don't think I will be breaking the blog habit anytime soon.

37

Dear Dog Owners,

FIRST OF ALL, I would like you to know I love dogs. I have had a dog in the past, I have done a fair amount of dogsitting, and I currently would like a dog.

That said, I am sick and tired of strange dogs running up to me off-leash on public trails. Would you come up to within half an inch of my body and then start rubbing against me in public without so much as an introduction? Didn't think so. Then why would you allow your dog to do this? I know, your dog is friendly, otherwise you wouldn't let him do this. Newsflash: I. Don't. Care. Your dog could be Miss America and I still wouldn't care, because when I am running along and an unfamiliar dog comes barreling at me while you stand there holding your travel coffee mug and saying nothing, I feel my stomach do a flip, and my whole body feels like it is on fire and my heart starts beating superfast, you know, like how you do when you randomly run into someone you used to date in the supermarket, which, thank god, I will probably never have to experience again because I moved a thousand miles from home and met the man I would eventually marry before I had time to really date anyone else.

I know you know the freaked-out feeling of which I speak. (You may also feel this way when you narrowly avoid a car accident or when you are just walking and for no reason your ankle rolls because your Dansko somehow got out from under you and you are like, "Oh crap, I am about to twist my ankle," and then when your ankle is fine you're like, "God, I hope no one saw me just totally lose my balance on my shoe.") So, please, quit acting like I am the one with the problem because I can't handle your friendly dog. It's downright scary when an animal you have never seen before is bounding toward you at a high rate of speed. The least you could do is say, "I'm sorry my dog scared you," but instead you act like I'm uptight. How about if I come running straight at you and stop when I am right in your face next time I see you, and when you act startled, I'll be all, "Hey, relax, dude! Geez, I'm just being *friendly!*"

See how you like it.

SINCERELY,
Pam

38

Farewell, Friend

DO YOU EVER wonder what you are doing here? Not sitting reading this. I mean the existential question of what is this all about and what is the point of being here on earth in this lifetime. Most of the time I am thinking about crossing things off my to-do list... Sending emails, remembering to take the laundry out of the washer before it molds, and stuff like that. Every once in a while I consider what my true purpose is, but not that much. It's kind of overwhelming because I don't have a really good answer right now. I was thinking about this on my bike ride today because I found out about the recent death of someone I used to know. What was his purpose in his relatively short life? He died, I could die, I will inevitably die, I am running out of time to figure out why I am really here and then make it happen...

I am not sure what to call this person. He was not exactly a friend and not exactly a patient of mine, but sort of both. I knew him when I worked in mental health. The place where I worked was a Clubhouse. No, not that kind of clubhouse. It's a day program for adults with chronic, severe mental illness. It is just as much a treatment center as it is a supportive community, a place where people with mental illness—who oftentimes cannot hold down a job, have a hard time maintaining friendships, and who may be estranged from their families—can go for support, camaraderie, and assistance with everything from understanding a bus schedule (OMG, I cannot believe I got paid to help people with that! I need a bus schedule tutor half the time myself) to getting their meds before their prescription runs out, to securing a part-time job. The patients or consumers are considered "members," and the staff's role is to find ways to let members use their skills and abilities to facilitate the daily operations of the clubhouse, including planning, preparing, and serving meals; advocating for mental health policy; running a thrift shop; planning social events; and fundraising. The idea is to engage people in something larger than themselves and to maximize their potential to live meaningful, productive lives in the community. Most of us do not realize that our everyday lives require us to be part of something bigger than ourselves, be it marriage, family, neighborhood, workplace, religious community, whatever. People with severe mental illness, on the other hand, do not necessarily have these resources, so the opportunities this day program gives them are truly unique and health promoting: Being part of something bigger than yourself means you have to wake up each morning. It means you have a purpose of some kind. We take it for granted, but having a purpose, even a purpose for one hour of each day, is life sustaining. Consider the alternative: You wake up with no one expecting you anywhere, anytime, at all, for anything. Just the idea of that kind of makes me want to crawl under the covers for a long, long time.

One of the members I am honored to have known passed away, and this is what I remember about him. He was a kind, gentle soul. He had a hard time in the world, coping with mental illness. He didn't have a job, he didn't have much contact with his family, and his mental stability was iffy. He had a huge heart and a bright smile. He had courage. People with mental illness are some of the bravest, strongest people I know. Simply put, they get shit on by society, and yet they have the fewest resources to better their situation. I know this is America, people need to pull themselves up by their bootstraps, blah blah blah, but I don't really want to hear it unless you have a severe, persistent chronic mental illness or a family member with one, otherwise you can't begin to understand what these people deal with on a daily basis. The endurance it must take just to keep on living boggles my mind. I had not talked to my friend in years, but when I heard the news of his passing I saw his smiling face in my mind and I thought this world just lost a beautiful soul. I hope that he is resting peacefully or that his soul might have the opportunity to live in harmony with a healthy mind. I imagine he must have struggled with his purpose on this earth, as most of us do. I cannot presume to say what it was. I can say that he will live in my memory as a source of inspiration, as one whose smile could light up a room. I feel lucky to have crossed paths with him.

39

The Yoga Scene

CAN SOMEONE TELL me when yoga became so ridiculously trendy?? I guess I have known it was hot for quite some time now, considering there was a yoga class available at my gym way back in 2002, when it was known as AC Fitness, or No-AC Fitness, as we no-so-affectionately dubbed it during the not-so-bearable North Carolina summers. And this was before hot yoga had caught on in that part of the country, so it wasn't in any way stylish; it was just hot, damp, and miserable. But the point is, although I mostly live under a rock, I knew yoga was gaining popularity, however, I had not realized to what extent until now.

So what happened was, it was Monday night and for some reason I was hell-bent on going to yoga. I think the last time I went to yoga was sometime last year, but the yoga bug bit me hard and I just had to get my om on and it had to be Monday. I got to the gym at 5:49 for the 6:00 class only to find the gym was closed for renovations. I was frustrated, but only briefly, for I live in one of the most crunchy-chic towns in the United States (yeah, crunchy chic, I just made that up). I knew that somewhere within a two-mile radius there had to be a yoga studio with a 6:00 class. So I booked it over to CorePower Yoga because I knew exactly where it was, and it was close.

It turned out to be the Chili's of yoga studios. Like, it's not bad, the price is reasonable, there's one in every major city, but why would you go there when you could go to a unique little venue with local flavor? Like, when I was in high school my friends and I loved Chili's. It was open late, we liked the chicken fajitas, there were bottomless diet cokes, and we liked the ambiance but we didn't really know any better. I suspect I would have really liked CorePower Yoga when I was in high school.

Except at that time there was no such thing as CorePower Yoga and no one I knew did yoga at all except me and my mom. On Monday nights we would go to this lady Joan's yoga class, which we heard about through my dad's cousin, who is a bird-watching, peace-loving, women's health activist type of person. In 1995, the way to find a yoga class was by asking this sort of person, for there was no World Wide Web, and your YMCA class schedule was not going to include yoga. The class was held on the third floor of a three-family house. There was no big shiny sign out front; it was just a space our teacher, Joan, rented for her classes. Joan reminded me of Mother Earth, if Mother Earth were a person. I was the youngest person there, and my mom was quite possibly the second youngest. We wore sweatpants or cotton Lycra leggings and T-shirts. The room was comfortably warm but not hot.

So, like, what happened in the last fifteen years??? I show up at yoga and it takes me several laps around the parking lot to finally find a spot, and then I walk into the studio and this girl at the cash register is telling me I can go to some vinyasa class in studio A or Yoga Sculpt in studio B. I pick Yoga Sculpt because it starts at 6:15 instead of 6:00, which allows me to change without being late. Then the girl tries to introduce me to the teacher of the class, and she's like, "Cool Yoga Dude, this is Pam, and she has never been here before!" Cool Yoga Dude totally ignored cash register girl, which was awkward. She tried again and he vaguely nodded, never taking his eyes off whatever it was he was doing at that moment. She was like, "Men totally can't multitask!" I smiled and nodded, as I can't say I disagree. I changed in the locker room, which was a total mob scene; however, they had mouthwash in big pump bottles with little disposable cups, which was cool.

I was astounded by all the skinny little women whom I would have classified as gym rats were we in a gym. I guess the more appropriate term would be yoga rat? That sounds weird, though. Anyway, I am observing all these hot young yoga rats, and I am like, "What is up with all these Lululemon'ed girls??" It looked like a yoga sorority. And then when I paused to stop thinking judgmental thoughts, I remembered I was wearing my unbelievably-awesome-worth-every-I-am-not-even-going-to-say-how-many-dollars-I-spent-on-them-because-my-mother-is-reading-this-and-she-would-have-a-cow-if-she-knew-but-they-are-reversible-so-it-is-like-having-two-pairs-of-pants-and-they-make-my-ass-look-perfect-Lululemon pants. And I remembered that I was in a sorority.

Anyway, I got to the class and looked around and saw everyone but me had a cool-looking thin towel over their mat. I figured it was a style thing. Meanwhile, Cool Yoga Dude was standing at the front of the room shirtless, with this hairstyle like none I have ever seen before. He had supershort hair except for a braid sticking out of the middle/top of his head. He didn't participate in the class, he just told us what to do. Between shavasanas and chaturangas I saw him go over to the thermostat and crank it way up. Soon my yoga mat was a big puddle of sweat. It resembled more of a slip-and-slide than a yoga mat, and I realized why everyone else had those towels. While I looked around to make fully sure I was truly the only person without a towel, I noticed I was one of the oldest people in the class. I realize I live in a college town, but aren't college students supposed to be busy studying or partying? If I were a college student now, I would probably be too busy stalking my crushes on Facebook and Twitter to make it to yoga class.

Anyway, class was good, I left so sweaty I felt as though I had taken a shower with my clothes on, and I think I opened up some chakras. It just made me miss the class I used to take with my mom back when yoga wasn't even cool. Or maybe I just missed being the youngest instead of one of the oldest.

40

How I Make It Look So Easy

HERE'S THE THING you need to know if you are going to get bangs: They're work. A lot of times, especially at my job, my patients ask me, "Do you have kids?" and I just smile and say no. But in my mind I am like, *Are you kidding me? I don't have a cat, I don't have a dog, I don't even have a pet rock. I am always, like. a thousand miles late on scheduling oil changes for my car. I have plants, but I do best with cacti and philodendrons (read: low maintenance). Anyways, I have freaking bangs, OK. That's what I can be responsible for right now. Bangs. They are more work than you think.*

About a year ago, in the spirit of trust and cooperation, in a zombielike rosemary-mint-shampoo-induced trance, I told my hairdresser she could do whatever she wanted. I ended up with bangs for the first time since 1991. And you know what? They were cute! They were fun! They totally went with my face and my new chin length hair! WHY HAD I BEEN AVOIDING BANGS SINCE THE SEVENTH GRADE!?!

No sooner had I experienced the thrill of lathering my newly shortened locks and the first post-shower shake of my new hair when I realized all the ramifications of my new coif... You have to blow bangs dry. Because if you don't, they don't even know they are bangs. They would act like regular hair if you let them, just going this way and that, trying to blend in with the rest of your hair, so you have to heat style them into submission or else put them back in a clip or a headband. Which is like the sound of a tree falling in the woods with no one to hear it—a complete waste.

Over the past year, I have learned not only how to properly maintain my bangs, but I have also learned what people mean when they talk about tuning out their spouse. I am not placing blame or naming names, but I am saying in our household there is one person who is frequently like, "Are my bangs out of control? Are they? What are they doing? I don't have a mirror. Seriously, are they crazy right now?" and another person who is neither answering nor making eye contact and is more than likely either watching *The Daily Show* or reading the business section. This person is prone to confirming having actually heard the bangs inquiry despite having fully ignored it, as evidenced by the propensity to ask at any given time, "Are my bangs out of control!?" in a way that is completely sarcastic and somewhat mocking.

You know who suffers the most in all of this? The bangs. And they don't suffer silently. They may wait quietly for a period of time, but inevitably they will exact revenge. Take this weekend for instance; Dan and I went camping. I didn't bring my blow dryer because I didn't know what the availability of electrical outlets would be like. As it turned out, they were plentiful. Each time I used the ladies room at our campground, the sight of the plethora of outlets taunted me and my bangs, which by Sunday morning were all but plastered to the top of my head, having been held down by some combination of a headband, head lamp, bike helmet, and/or fleece hat for forty-eight hours straight.

Monday came and my bangs seemed to mock me, as if to say, "You ignore us, we ignore you!" Despite having washed and blown them out on Sunday night, I awoke Monday, having pressed snooze no fewer than ten times, with bangs pointing north, south, east, and west. They didn't go with my business casual outfit. With just ten minutes to get out of the house and still make it to work on time, I plugged in my slim yet powerful Chi flatiron. It heated up with warp speed while my bangs were forming what would turn out to be an army of resistance. For as soon as I released the steaming-hot straightening tool from my hair, instead of the totally under control look my hairdresser so easily achieved in the salon, I had bangs that were poker straight, resting at a 45-degree angle to my head. I tried to get them to lie flat, but they would not retreat. I backpedaled, quickly wetting them and blasting them with my blow dryer, to no avail. At a 45-degree angle they remained, their proverbial heels digging steadfast into the mud/my scalp.

I came to the breakfast table armed with a battle plan and a barrette in my pocket. If my bangs did not relax down by the time I got to work, I would clip them back. As I inhaled my oatmeal, Dan happened to look up from the paper. For what might have been the first time since I have known him, he took a good look at my bangs. He stared for a moment. "Your bangs. They're really… straight." I had kept my cool up to then, but everyone has a breaking point. "I KNOW!! I KNOW THEY ARE STRAIGHT. THEY ARE STRAIGHT AND THEY ARE IN A DIFFERENT ZIP CODE THAN MY FOREHEAD!!! I HAVE NO TIME FOR THIS!!! I AM GOING TO BE LATE FOR WORK AND MY BANGS ARE OUT OF CONTROL. I have a barrette just in case." Moved by the gravity of the situation, Dan laughed hysterically and finally for once agreed, "Your bangs are totally out of control." I wanted to ask him if he was sure but I knew that he was and that would be like asking if your butt was eating your too-tight jeans when you can totally feel them giving you a wedgie as you ask the question, so I said nothing and accepted that my bangs were a disaster that even Dan could recognize.

It was kind of worth it just to get Dan to acknowledge my bangs. I think he is starting to get how hard it is to be me.

41

It's Happening

I HAVE MADE a few observations regarding myself of late that… concern me.

1. A COUPLE of weeks ago, Dan asked me about a laundry basket in the corner of our room that was about three-quarters full. "What is this doing here?" I explained it was a load of clothes that I was getting ready to put in the wash. Then I watched as he casually dropped a green T-shirt into the basket.

"What are you doing? That is a load of blacks. Save that T-shirt for the next load; I am doing colors soon."

He looked at me as if I had just told him I was going to save water and run a load of wash in cat piss instead.

"Seriously, Pam?"

"What?"

"Does it really matter if the blacks are with the blacks? You used to just throw in a load of whatever whenever we had enough for a full laundry basket. You never even separated lights and darks. What is this all about?"

He never used to eat raw daikon radishes, but that's a whole other story.

"I just think the colors will stay brighter if we wash similar colors together."

Dan shook his head and I proceeded with my load of blacks, then I collected a load of brights, and finally a load of sheets and towels. I silently wondered when I had become my mother, the original laundry nazi, demanding that denims go together, reds and pinks go together, etc., leaving you to wonder when you unwittingly threw a favorite yellow T-shirt in the hamper whether you'd be able to wear it again in the next eight to ten weeks, should it take that long for a full load of yellows and oranges to accumulate, finally granting them admission to the washing machine.

2. TUESDAY, I was on my way to the gym before work when I finally got sick of looking at this little stain in our toilet bowl. You would think a person would get used to it, but I haven't. It's not a major thing; it's a light gray spot right at the base of the bowl, where the bowl borders the hole where all the water flushes. I always think the cleaning lady will get it but she never does, which is weird because she does such a thorough job with everything else. And so the interplay of factors, including a subtle desire to procrastinate the workout, an overt desire to avoid going outside in subzero weather, and what had become a chronic irritation with the gray spot, led to the perfect storm; in the moments just before dawn, while Dan slept soundly, I scrubbed the mark with the enthusiasm of a monkey on crack. Vigorously, I applied pressure to the scrubby from a variety of angles, all to no avail. My patience wore thin as I continued to pump the scrubby up and down at a perpendicular angle to the bowl, then again at a 45-degree angle to the bowl, and then repeated the sequence again. I was beginning to understand why our cleaning lady had never gotten the bowl

100 percent clean. It occurred to me I might be better off getting in there with some bleach and an old toothbrush when suddenly I was lunging forward, my face headed directly for the bowl. I righted my balance just inches before my nose was submerged in the water. I hadn't realized I was putting nearly all of my body weight into my endeavor until my equilibrium was suddenly altered by the stick of my toilet scrubber breaking cleanly in half.

"Damn it!" I cried.

"What?" Dan called from the bedroom.

"Nothing. I just broke our toilet brush trying to clean the toilet."

Did I really just say that? How did this happen to me? When did I become someone who would exert violent force on a cleaning instrument? We weren't even anticipating company. I am, at heart, a total slob. My mom is the neat freak. I take after my dad! I didn't even know myself anymore. Worse, I was pondering this fact without even having had so much as a sip of coffee yet. Also, my heart was heavy with disappointment that I had broken this particular scrubby because of its sentimental value, which sounds ridiculous but is true. What happened was I put it on our wedding gift registry at the last minute, and it was given to us by my best friend's in-laws, which was just so sweet because they weren't even invited to our wedding, and, actually, I have not seen them since my best friend's wedding, which was in 2005, but apparently I made a really good impression on my friend's mother-in-law, who apparently asks after me often and who was kind enough to think of me and Dan and buy us the matching toilet brush and garbage can from our registry, even though she had not seen or heard from me in five years. So you can see why I was touched by the gesture.

3. I HAVE developed a habit of taking Dan's coat from the living room chair and hanging it on a hanger in the coat closet.

Sometimes I wonder when I started caring where other people left their stuff. Because, really, when I think about all the cool things I could have done with my life, all the degrees I might have earned, all the books and short stories I could have written, all the pies and cakes I could have baked, the African children I could have adopted and cared for had I only not wasted all the hours I have spent over the years looking for my keys/wallet/purse/the library books I meant to return on time/my lunch/my jacket/the sweater I was dying to wear/whatever because I had misplaced them or because they were obscured by a mountain of other stuff that I never bothered to put away, well, it really is just pathetic. And sometimes I think about the shrill tone of my mom's yell circa 1995, to which sometimes I would yell back "What?" and just as often pretend as if I did not hear her, knowing her next cry would be "You left your shoes in the den! Take them upstairs or you will find them in the garbage!" In my room, I would roll my eyes, knowing she would never actually make good on her threat, wondering why she didn't have something better to do than get pissy about my shoes.

4. I FINALLY changed my last name. I got my new driver's license, new social security card, new ID badge at work, new ATM card, the whole megillah. What really thrills me about taking Dan's last name is that now I can use Sinel as my middle name. I never had a middle name before, but I always wanted one. My dad is fond of saying he and my mom couldn't afford middle names for us back when we were little. I used to act like I didn't believe him, and I knew he was just kidding, but I actually wasn't sure for a long time. (I believed in Santa till I was, like, ten and he didn't even come to our house.) Anyway, it's been kind of an adjustment to a new signature. The worst part is making the cursive *r* in Moore and making sure it doesn't come out looking like an *n*.

The best part is the flourish with which I sign my middle initial, S. (I love having a middle initial!!) It took me a few times to realize I had done this before. Then it all came rushing back to me… I used to forge my mom's signature in middle school, which has a big old S as the middle initial. For the life of me, I have no earthly idea why I would have done that. Despite having been a snot (see above), I was actually a pretty good kid. I got good grades, I was rarely absent, never tardy, and I always turned in my homework on time and, except for math, mostly correct, so why I was pretending I was my mother doesn't make any sense to me now. But what I remember was the fun I had signing her middle initial, which also happens to be an S. The curves and swirls of S were a roller coaster for my pen.

WHAT THIS ALL means is that I think (fear—no, not really fear, I love you, Mom, but well, yes, maybe fear a little, but in a good way) what this all adds up to is that I am turning into my mother. Stay tuned. Other signs to watch for include steam cleaning the kitchen counter and adopting a stray Chihuahua mutt (the latter of which is actually my secret dream).

42

Note to Self: Learn to Read

ON FRIDAY MORNING, I was so jazzed to start my day by putting a pork shoulder in the crock pot. My mom has been talking about this dish for weeks, about how easy it is, how the meat just falls off the bone, and that I have to try it, so I finally went to the supermarket, got myself a nice big piece of pork shoulder and started getting excited about the taste of tender pork. According to my mom, the way to do it is to put it in the crock pot with some loosely chopped onions and a jar of barbecue sauce. And P.S., that is barbecue with a *c*. I thought it was a *q* and I could not figure out why spellcheck was calling me out... I guess you read *BBQ* so much you think the word must have a *q*; it doesn't. Just fyi. Anyway, according to the Internet, it is best to first braise the pork and then make little slits and stuff it with garlic (I did this with brisket once and it was fan-fucking-tastic, and I rarely use the f-word, so you know I am SERIOUS). The Internet also talked about adding red wine, chicken broth, and some other stuff, so I did a variation on everyone's recipe and did my own eclectic thing, with the braising, the garlic, onions, some wine, a little broth. It was also the perfect opportunity to use up the miscellaneous five-ounce bottles of half-empty barbecue sauce we have had in the pantry for practically ever. I poured it all in the crock pot, shut the lid, turned it to low, and went about my busy day with daydreams of tender pork intermittently penetrating my consciousness.

Evening came and I tasted my aromatic concoction to test for doneness. No sooner had I swallowed it than my throat began to burn and my eyes smarted with tears. What the Hades!?

"Dan, taste this!!?"

Dan tasted it. I should say it was probably not very nice of me not to even warn him, considering Dan is more of a mild spicy person while I am more of a medium to very spicy person as far as our food preferences, but I was collecting data. Dan confirmed my findings. He sort of lurched his neck forward and opened his eyes wide as he swallowed.

"What did you do?"

"I don't know. Why is this so spicy!? Oh my god, I don't even know if we can eat this!"

"I was wondering why all the hot sauce bottles were empty."

I paused. What was Dan talking about?

"Hot sauce?? That was barbecue sauce!!"

Dan maintained it was hot sauce and that he likes to eat it on his eggs.

"But I've never seen you do that. I thought we never ate that stuff. What the hell? That is barbecue sauce!! I swear to god. If it's not barbecue sauce, why does it say *Barbecue Sauce* right on the label!???"

Dan said nothing but took one of the empty bottles and brought it up to my face. I read the words, stupefied.

"HARRY'S HABENERO HOT SAUCE!? ARE YOU FUCKING KIDDING ME!? I THOUGHT THIS WAS BARBECUE SAUCE. JESUS H. CHRIST. I HAVE RUINED THIS MEAL!!!!"

I glared at Dan.

"How come you never told me that was hot sauce??"

Dan looked at me and paused for a moment. Slowly he replied, "I guess I thought you would read the label."

I looked at him, disgusted.

"Are you seriously mad at me?"

"No. OK, yes, I was. But I shouldn't have been. I am just mad at the whole situation." Yes, OK, I admit it. I admit it to the whole world. I was mad at my husband because I added half a cup worth of hot sauce to the crock pot pork shoulder. I am both crazy and mean, the worst combination.

I added a cup of chicken broth, hoping it would dilute the mouth-burning flavor, to no avail.

I thought serving it with a side of rice might neutralize the heat, but I was wrong there as well. It was indeed tender, but the only thing I could really taste was hot. I wouldn't say I am a foodie (no doy, right?) but even I know hot is not a flavor.

Sufficiently satiated for our date to the Boulder International Film Festival, which is actually special because that was where we went for our first date, we grabbed some minty gum as we left the house well in advance, knowing we would need to allow ample time to park, to wait in line, and to get toward the front of the line so I might be availed the opportunity to avoid sitting behind a tall person, which was what happened to me at the noontime showing of *The First Grader*. I said it was a busy day; I didn't say I wasn't enjoying it.

We ran into our friends in line for the movie and because they were ahead of us, they said they'd save us seats. It seemed so perfect. As we neared the front of the line, Dan mentioned his stomach was hurting because of how spicy the pork was. Unlike our first date, I got totally defensive and I was like, "How do you know that's why your stomach hurts? Maybe it's because you ate too much of it." Which was wrong of me to say on so many levels.

The truth is one bite of it was far too much, and Dan was exceptionally kind to even give it a chance. Dan told me he knew it was because of the spicy factor because his stomach had never felt like this before. I followed our friends to the upper level of Boulder Theater and turned around and Dan was gone. I looked all around but I couldn't find him. And he didn't even have his phone. Did he go to the bathroom? Why would he go to the bathroom without at least mentioning it? He disappeared. I did another loop around the theater, a little bit frantic. I was getting pissed. Would it have killed him to tell me, "Hon, I am going to the men's room." What if he was not in the men's room? I needed to test out my movie seat and make sure no one too tall was sitting in front of me before it was too late to find a new seat. Where was he??

Finally he appeared.

"Where did you go!?" I asked, not warmly. Dan looked a little frazzled as he explained they wouldn't let him in because his ticket (the one I had printed online) was for the wrong movie and we were supposed to be at the church across the street for our movie. Why they scanned my ticket and let me in was a mystery but obviously a mistake. He said he called me from some phone but my phone was off and they wouldn't let him in to find me until he gave them his driver's license for collateral.

What movie was this that we were in, I wanted to know. Why was this not *Into Eternity*? How could our movie be anywhere other than here? Dan assured me it did not matter but that we needed to get our act together and go to the church so we could see the movie we actually had tickets for. We bade our friends a rushed good-bye, Dan got his license back, and we booked it over to the church.

"I can't believe it's at the church!" I cried, indignant.

"Pam, it says the location right on the ticket."

Indeed it did. Right on the ticket I had printed out an entire day ago. The ticket I could have read but didn't. This whole reading thing was turning out to be the bane of my existence. Instead of being mad at having to read, I redirected my anger at Dan.

"I was so pissed that you just disappeared from me! I had no idea where you were."

"Pam, are you seriously mad at me?"

"Well…I was. But I'm not. No. I'm mad we are now not going to be early for this movie and I might have to sit behind someone tall again."

It turned out we had great seats, I was able to see fine in between the heads of the two people sitting directly in front of me, and the movie was depressing but really good. Also, this time I knew what a documentary was (yes, there was a time when I didn't even know what a documentary was), which was definitely a plus.

Thank you, Dan, for three awesome years, for being your awesome self and enjoying another BIFF movie with me, and for discovering I have the capacity to be alternately crazy, angry, defensive, impatient, and illiterate all in one evening and for loving me anyway.

43

Dos and Don'ts for Working from Home

HAVE YOU EVER dreamed of working from home? Have you fantasized about the traffic you could avoid, the comfort of staying in your pj's all day long, imagined the money you could save by eating lunch at home every day? I recently saw something… I cannot for the life of me remember what it was but somebody (a teenager, I think) called somebody (their parent?) a "dream crusher." This phrase comes to mind now as I say that I believe, with every fiber of my being, that working from home sucks. I've been doing it part-time for nearly three years, and in these short thirty-one months I have learned a few things that I would like to share.

If you have to work from home, here is the Original Pamela S. Moore List of Dos and Don'ts:

1. Do get dressed. It helps trick your mind into thinking something important (e.g., work) is happening or could potentially happen, and this may (no guarantees here, just may) help you actually make something (e.g., work) happen. It sucks that

no one will get to appreciate your cute outfit, much like the sound of a tree falling in the woods with no one to hear it, but you must get over this or see #7.

2. Don't take a break just to put a load of clothes in the wash. Because inevitably you will notice all the sad, abandoned clothes that were left in the dryer/on the drying rack and feel that now is the perfect time to fold them and, heck, while you are at it, put them away, and jeez wouldn't you know, by the time you are done with all that the wash cycle is over and your clothes need to be moved to the dryer, and if you are going down to the basement anyway, you might as well bring down another load of dirty clothes to throw in. And since you are in the basement, it wouldn't hurt to see what's in the chest freezer that you can defrost for tonight's dinner. And then you wonder how your five-minute stretch break turned into a forty-five-minute break.

3. Do spend ten dollars on the web application Freedom. It lets you make the Internet totally inaccessible for however long you tell it to.

4. Click on Freedom and use it. Click on it before you start working, not after you have checked Gmail, Facebook, HuffPost, and all your favorite blogs and then realize it's been an hour since you sat down and now you have to get up anyway to microwave your coffee. Going to the kitchen will only lead you to decide to empty the dishwasher and to finally collect the last three days' worth of *Daily Camera*s that have been littering the kitchen table and drop them in the recycle bin. This will mysteriously find you back at the computer no sooner than twenty minutes later.

5. Do not answer the phone!!! Do not answer for your sister, mother, friends, or anything nonwork related. You must create the illusion that you are not always available even though

you technically are! Answer only for your spouse, but only if it's because you would start acting like a stark raving mad clingy lunatic if he/she didn't pick up when you called.

6. Do not check Amazon just to see if they have one item. OF COURSE THEY HAVE IT. THEY HAVE FREAKING EVERYTHING. That is why they are Amazon, not some website you've never even heard of. And P.S., if Amazon doesn't have it, eBay probably will. Whatever it is, you can put it in your cart later. Because if you start with one item, thirty minutes later you will have that one item plus five others in your cart, which is fine because it is all tax-deductible work-related stuff BUT YOU STILL HAVE ACCOMPLISHED NO WORK, and don't try to say it's OK because all the stuff in your cart is relevant to your professional development because you won't give a crap at 8 p.m. when you wish you were already home from the gym and having dinner but instead you are just starting your workout, which you could have started two hours ago had you not been dicking around when you were supposed to be working.

7. Do go to a coffee shop, but you must go with the expectation that someone loud and annoying will sit practically on top of you. Bring headphones and develop the ability to listen to music while working if you don't already know how to do that.

8. Do NOT schedule coffee dates, lunch plans, massages, other appointments, or stuff that you would normally do on a day off. You are WORKING. Even if you don't get as much done as you wanted, let it be the fault of the Internet, not your own stupid fault for actively making plans not to work.

9. Have a goal and meet it. Create a reasonable goal of something you know you can accomplish by day's end and make it happen, even if it takes you longer than you thought it

would. This lets you tell yourself "I mean business!" and will allow you to take yourself seriously now and in the future.

10. Create a reward system. I once told myself I could not under any circumstances get the iPhone, which I had been obsessed with for months (Was it worth it? I am not sure. The phone is great—it's AT&T that I could do without, but that is a whole other topic.) until I got my work done. Often I simply tell myself, *If you do the work now, you won't have to do it later*, and this is sufficient incentive. I would have to work a lot more if I bought myself an iPhone or the equivalent every time I got something done.

44

He Said, She Said

RESEARCH HAS SHOWN that women speak up to three times more words per day than men speak on average. But is it true? That sounds like a big discrepancy. Well, if numbers, figures, and statistics aren't your thing, here is a little qualitative research for you, based on a non-scientific study I performed over the last twenty-four hours.

This morning, when I was on the phone with my sister, she mentioned she had called me last night. She continued, "I thought I was calling your cell phone because in my phone I have my contacts mixed up and I have your Skype phone as your cell number and your cell number as your Skype number. So I didn't realize I was calling your Skype phone, and then Dan picked up, and I thought it was you, because I thought I was calling your cell, so I was like 'Are you okay?' Because it didn't sound like you at all. And he was like 'I'm fine, what's up?' And I still thought you sounded really weird, like maybe you were sick or something but I was like 'Not much, what are you doing?' and he said, 'Cooking,' and then I realized it was Dan, not you, and he thought I was you!"

On the other hand, when I returned from the gym yesterday and walked through the door, Dan called out from the kitchen, "Your sister called."

45

Dear Guardian Angel,

I JUST WANTED to say thanks. I don't know why you picked me, maybe it's because I need you so much? Dan sometimes shakes his head and asks me, "How did you live before you met me?" Not because he is arrogant or anything like that, far from it! Just because he is pretty responsible, and I am...not irresponsible, but just more, I don't know what you call it. "Scattered" evokes the image of a lady running errands with a stray curler left on the back of her head. Not scattered. And not disorganized...just needing a lot of Post-it notes or something.

It feels like every time I turn around, I am losing something or forgetting something. Like yesterday, we were about to get on the highway to head to Boston Logan when I realized I had left my phone at my parents'. That would have sucked if I'd forgotten it!!! Anyway, Dan doesn't realize perhaps that, yes, he helps me a lot, but even before there was Dan, there was you, my angel, making sure my whole life didn't go to hell in a handbasket and, at the very least, keeping me safe from identity theft, just because I am a bit careless at times.

I don't mean to be cocky, but after more than thirty years of this, I worry less because I just sort of know you will take care of me. I know, you are shaking your head like, "Worry less!? The best part of all this is watching you curse and dump out your purse, like, ten times while you flip out!" Did you think it was funny this week, watching me lose my shit when I couldn't find my license?! Honestly, I don't blame you if you thought it was a riot, watching me make a dozen phone calls, photocopy our engagement and wedding announcements, get my mom to dig out my birth certificate, and attempt to get to the airport extra early (which I would have if we hadn't had to go back for my cell phone) in case I needed time to convince the TSA of my identity, only to find my license had been sitting at the Southwest office at Denver International Airport for over a week, even though they were all "We would have mailed it to our Dallas headquarters within twenty-four hours of finding it"!? Seriously, I was not only dreading having to spend this morning at the DMV, but also my license picture with my new last name turned out CUTE, and I wasn't sure a new pic would be as attractive.

But then there was that time, remember in 2008, when Dan and I went to Philly for my friends' wedding, and I must have dropped my license in security, who knows… I ended up getting a new one right away (with an even cuter pic than the first one), and then the airline mailed me my old license within a weeks' time. That was sweet because I had a spare ID, which came in handy more than once.

What about that time in graduate school that I had a bit too much fun celebrating the end of the semester the night before my flight home for Christmas break!? Remember how I passed out in my clothes, and I woke up when my friend walked into my apartment the next morning and I was still asleep even though it was time for her to drive me to the airport!? I was so frazzled I forgot my purse, but the beauty of the whole thing was my drivers' license was still in the pocket of the pants I never bothered to change!

Which reminds me of the time in Vegas I had to return to Pure the next night when they opened again because I had left without closing out the tab (don't ask), and after a lot of problems, the main one being I was having a hard time even locating the entrance of the club because Caesars Palace is BIG and my sense of direction is BAD, and then when I finally got everything sorted out, they returned my credit card AND my license, which I didn't even know I had lost!

Also, thanks for making sure no one stole my huge leather purse, which included my wallet and my passport when I left it at that cafe in Costa Rica. OMG, were you dying when Dan and I drove two hours to return the rental car, it was POURING down rain, and I had to tell Dan we had to go back to that place we ate lunch, the place whose name started with an *M*, except we didn't remember anything else except that it was on the left-hand side of the road, because I totally forgot my purse!? And then I had to make Dan drive most of the way, even though he'd already been driving basically all day, because I am a total grandma when it comes to night driving!? It wasn't funny at the time, but it's kind of funny now. The best part was when I walked into the place and no one spoke English, but the guy at the bar pointed at me and gestured about a big square, and then I nodded, and he brought out my bag from the back, completely intact!

Or what about that time I was working out at the Wellness Center, like, a hundred years ago when I lived in Chapel Hill, and when I got back to my car, my purse, which was supposed to have been in the car, was totally not there and I realized I had left my passenger window wide open, and I wigged out because obviously someone had reached in and just grabbed it. Remember how I was feeling like such an idiot when I went up to the front desk to borrow the phone to call the police, and then the reception lady held up the floral bag and she was like, "Is this it?" Some awesome person saw that my window was wide open with the purse on the passenger side so they brought it in for safekeeping.

And that same purse—you must love that purse as much as I do (except can you help me find the matching mini-bag that goes with it; I haven't seen that in years!), because of that time I left it at the Starbucks at Wadsworth and Alameda. That was crazy. The whole day went by and it was, like. 9 p.m. when I realized it was missing and that was the last place I'd had it, at, like, 8:30 that morning. I called up and sure enough they had it, but I didn't feel like schlepping forty-fives minutes to get it that night, when I would practically be down the street the next morning for work. I felt the Starbucks lady had a nice vibe about her and that my purse would be safe till the next morning, and when I got there the next morning, before I could even say "Double-shot Americano with a shot of steamed soy in a sixteen-ounce cup," the lady looked at me and yelled "Flower Power!" (a nod to the wacky flower print on the bag), as if I were just another regular, even though that was only the second time I'd ever been in there. As usual, nothing was even missing!

And don't think I forgot about the time I lost my hospital ID badge last fall. It wasn't just my ID badge but also my Eco-Pass and a nearly full twenty-dollar cash card for the cafeteria that I lost. You have been so good to me, but I never expected you would figure out a way for someone to have returned all that stuff to the emergency room and that the receptionist there would have contacted me within twenty-four hours, before I even had time to go to HR for a new badge and to try to beg for a new Eco-Pass!

And the bus pass I lost in graduate school—that was worth, like, two hundred dollars and somehow I lost it... On the very day I was ready to bite the bullet and buy a new one, someone from…was it the Safety office? Who knows… They called me to tell me someone had turned in my bus pass.

And that whole thing with my cell phone—remember when I left it in the hotel in Silverthorne and I worried I would never see it again, but then the hotel guy eventually mailed it to me and I did get it, albeit ten days later… That was a close one!

Anyway, all of this to say I haven't forgotten all the times you have come to my aid, helping to return all the important things I have lost track of. Thank you!!!

LOVE,
Pam

46

Pregnancy Top Six List

IF I HAD known how awesome being pregnant was, I might have done this sooner... I'm not kidding. This is great.

TOP SIX AWESOME THINGS ABOUT MY PREGNANCY (AND, YES, I KNOW THESE LISTS ARE TYPICALLY TOP TEN BUT PLEASE SEE #5)

1. I have gotten more comments from strangers on how great I look in the past few weeks than I ever have in my whole entire life. And I'm not including strangers in bars, because that doesn't count. I'm talking about the creepy guy at Borders in Chapel Hill in 2003 and the hot tattoo guy from the Denver Public Library, and, OK, while tattoos are not my thing, let's just say Dan was lucky he met me two days before tattoo guy did. And I don't care that almost all the people who happen to think I look so great right now are women. Doesn't matter. They're strangers and they are saying these lovely things that just make my day. I am an equal opportunity compliment taker, thank you.

2. For once I am not rejecting outfits because my stomach sticks out too much, wondering if my stomach sticks out too much, wearing things that disguise my stomach, or trying to suck my stomach in. My stomach has nowhere to go but out, and I don't care!! And the best part is it's rock hard! My stomach has never been so hard. OK, flat and hard would be awesome but one out of two ain't bad.
3. For the first time in my Boulder life, people are impressed with my athleticism. Because running six marathons and completing two Ironmans aren't a big deal around here. But bike ten miles pregnant to volunteer at your triathlon club's duathlon with a baby bump and suddenly you're a lean mean machine. Teach a spin class with a bun in the oven and you're an obsessive athlete. (And P.S., pregnant or not, just because you are teaching doesn't mean you are necessarily doing all the things you are telling your class to do.) At Zumba tonight, I was practically a celebrity. And I don't care if my fans were middle-aged ladies. To reiterate, I'm all about equal opportunity compliment taking.
4. You get to buy new clothes. Actually, you HAVE to buy new clothes. Forced clothes shopping… I couldn't have even made up such a wonderful thing if I tried!!!
5. I am GROWING A HUMAN IN MY BODY.
6. No need to feel guilty re: sleeping in, going to bed early, bailing early on social endeavors, eating whatever looks good, skipping a workout, or yawning at work (see #5).

47

Birth Report: Sweet Pea

THE BABY FINALLY decided to make her grand appearance… I've been busy snuggling her, gazing at her, and nursing her. Also, I've been on the phone a lot, catching up with friends. Today one of my friends and I had this exchange.

> Friend: What was your labor like?
>
> Me: Oh my god, it was epic. I was being pretty patient overall, as far as being waaaay past my due date, but by Thursday I was losing it. Wednesday night I thought my water broke, and then I went to the doctor and they said everything looked great and if my water broke, the baby would come anytime. Then I went to my midwife and she tested me and it turned out my water really didn't break.

At that point, my mom had been visiting for more than ten days and we were starting to grate on each other, I still didn't have a baby, and I was having a major, major meltdown. Every visit we'd had since about thirty-eight weeks, I asked my midwife if she thought I would have the baby soon and she kept saying she didn't think I was "grumpy enough" yet. I guess Thursday I hit the mark on the grump-o-meter... My mom and I went to a reading by an author I really like, and as we were leaving the bookstore, I had some intense back pain, which turned out to be the beginning of labor. I was able to go home and rest, but by about 1 a.m. I was totally awake, and the contractions were gradually getting stronger and closer together.

My midwife came at about 6 a.m. and things were moving along, until I started throwing up everything I tried to take in, which was mostly water and Recharge. When there was nothing left, I was dry heaving. I felt like I had the flu. I was sweating and freezing and basically totally miserable, even between contractions, by Friday afternoon. I wanted to go to the hospital and get some anti-nausea medication and an epidural, but I could not conceive of even getting dressed or getting in the car, so that was not really an option. Also, I reminded myself the whole point of having a baby at home was to avoid the hospital. I did not want a doctor poking a needle in my back...except I was starting to think maybe I did. I also didn't want to have a C-section... But then again at least that would mean the damn baby would finally be out of me. I never said these things aloud, mostly because I barely had it in me to talk, except to say "puke" (which was code for "Pass me the puke pot, I'm about to puke"), "don't touch me" (mostly directed at Dan), or "stop talking" (mostly directed at my mom).

Sometime Friday evening, I started to be able to hold down liquids, and then things started to move along a bit better. Of course this is all relative, as the baby wasn't actually born until Saturday at 3:30 a.m. When she finally crowned, I thought I was going to die—I never felt pain like that in my life, but I was relieved because at least the hard part was over. Except it wasn't. I was on my hands and knees in the birth tub and my midwife was urging me to stand up. Huh!? I thought the baby was supposed to slide on out now, but that was not the case. I stood up and leaned on Dan, and then I felt what really was the worst pain in the world.

Apparently our Sweet Pea had her hands up at her face and the cord was around her neck, so the midwife needed to do some fancy manipulation to get her out safely and quickly. Finally, she was out and in my lap, just staring at us, and I could not believe we had created this perfect little baby. Who actually wasn't that little, at eight pounds, eight ounces.

Friend: **Wow.**
Me: **Yeah, it was intense.**
Friend: **I can't imagine that kind of pain.**
Me: **I couldn't either, there's no way to describe it. It's unbelievable.**
Friend: **So would you do a home birth again?**
Me: **Oh, yes, definitely!**

48

Wanted: More Arms

MY BROTHER HAS a theory that people, like dogs, should have tails. It sounds a little funny (like, weird funny, not ha-ha funny), but it actually makes a lot of sense; you could wag your tail to show you were happy, or use it to hold an extra drink, for example. You would have to totally redesign your wardrobe to make this theory a reality (my observation, not my brother's), but it would be worth it.

I was reminded of my brother's theory today when Sweet Pea and I went to my favorite coffee shop. I'm no expert on parenting, but I will say this: I think nature mixed up when the octopus got eight arms and human mothers only got two.

It was inevitable that Sweet Pea would have a meltdown in public, and up until today I have avoided this scenario by a) not going out, or b) going out for very limited periods. Today, Dan and I were on a walk with Sweet Pea. For more than an hour, she slept peacefully in her stroller. Until the moment we approached the coffee shop where I intended to grab a drink, at which point Dan was to continue on to his office while I planned to sit with our baby and enjoy my coffee. As if on cue, just as Dan bade me farewell, Sweet Pea let out a shriek, which led to a sob, and within seconds she was in complete freak-out mode.

Dan looked at me apologetically as he had to be at a meeting in just a few minutes. I was like, "No problem, I've got this, go ahead," mainly because there were a ton of people sitting on the patio of the coffee shop and it would have been embarrassing to wrap my body around my husband's shin and beg him not to leave me alone with our screaming newborn. I assured him there was a changing table in the bathroom and I would deal with her in there. I've been to this coffee shop a thousand times. I could have sworn there was a changing table in the bathroom. But then again, before now, I didn't really care one way or the other if there was one or not.

There wasn't.

So I put Sweet Pea on a copy of *The Onion* that happened to be resting on the countertop and checked her diaper. Definitely wet. I found a hook that was about two feet higher than my head and attempted to hang my diaper bag there and then realized there was no way I could access any of the contents if I placed it there, so I put it on the floor. The dirty public bathroom floor. Holding my squirmy, crying, red-faced baby in one arm, I fished through the bag to find the handy zipper pouch that holds the little pad you put the baby on to avoid placing the baby directly on the floor in times like these. With the baby wedged between my body and my upper arm, her arms and legs flailing as she wailed, I clumsily used both hands to unzip the pouch and unfold the pad because, trust me, it's basically impossible to unzip or to unfold anything with just one hand. I lowered the baby to the mat and changed her diaper. Of course, I had forgotten to put a disposable diaper on her before we left, so with one hand on the baby to keep her from rolling onto the bathroom floor, I used my other hand to scrunch her soaked cloth diaper into a ball with the urine-soaked part on the inside and shove it into the little pouch, making every possible effort to avoid getting my hand damp with baby urine. Even with two hands, this would have been hard. With one hand, I was just barely able to do it.

Once she was diapered up and ready to go, I stood up and realized my Achilles tendons ached from kneeling on the bathroom floor that whole time. I really wanted to wash my hands, but there was no way to access the sink while holding Sweet Pea. The octopus thing is making sense now, right? How awesome would that be—one arm for the baby, one arm to hold the diaper bag, while one arm can dig through it to find stuff, which leaves you with five free arms for miscellaneous activities like wiping crud off your baby's face…

Before I exited the bathroom, Sweet Pea started screaming again. I sat down in the first patio chair I saw, surrounded by people sipping coffee, facing a parking lot. I rearranged my scarf, pulled up my shirt, and hoped that between the scarf and Sweet Pea's head this was a G-rated venture. You can imagine the pressure I felt to position Sweet Pea, undo my bra, deal with the nursing pad (P.S. How come no one told me how annoying it is to have leaky tatas!? Not that it would have changed anything, but still), and get her to latch, ASAP, all while maintaining some degree of decency. Should nursing in public continue in this way, you will either find me switching to formula, developing an ulcer, or with the skills to work under pressure commonly seen in firefighters and Navy Seals.

Sweet Pea sensed my terror tension and accordingly interrupted her sucking with regular intervals of sobbing, lest I were to become at all cocky about my mothering skills.

When she was finally done nursing and her crying had faded to a whimper, I placed her back in the stroller, which began a whole new cascade of sobs. Fun Fact: She didn't actually shed any tears, as newborns don't have tear ducts. But trust me, you don't need to see tears to know when your two-and-a-half-week-old is pissed off. I gave her a pacifier and moved the stroller back and forth a little, and soon her little eyes started to close. I exhaled.

Then I leaned in close to her face and softly asked, "Can Mommy please get a coffee now?" And then I thought for a second. Nothing about motherhood has really been like I thought it would be. I never thought I would randomly check to make sure the baby was still breathing (I do). I said I would never use a white noise machine to get the baby to sleep (I would try anything). I never imagined I would change all the words to "Party Anthem" to sing to my baby ("Every day I'm snugglin'… Every day I'm sucklin… Every day I'm cuddlin….")

I realize one should never say never, but I also said I would never ask my kid stuff like, "Can I get a coffee?" Seriously, who asks their child's permission to get a drink? Not this mama. I got up in my baby's face again. "Just to clarify, I'm getting a coffee."

A mocha never tasted so good.

49

New Mom Goes to Great Lengths for Alone Time

I FOUND THAT a gum graft was just the thing to cure my mama blues. See, I was supposed to have oral surgery about this time last year. But then I found out I was pregnant, so I ended up rescheduling it. Stay with me, I promise this will make sense.

I was apprehensive. You see, this wasn't my first rodeo. I had my first gum graft in 1988. What I remember about it was asking my dad how much it would cost. He told me five hundred dollars. That was the equivalent of a thousand visits from the tooth fairy. Did my family have this kind of money? Tentatively, I asked my dad, "Can we afford it?" He told me that even if I only lived to be sixty, the procedure would average out to ten dollars per year, and so, no, it was not something to worry about. By the way, times have changed. In 2012, I would have to live to be about 183 for this to be such an economical procedure, and what's worse is that this time around, Mom and Dad aren't footing the bill.

What I should have worried about was not the financial expense but the pain. I remember sitting in the periodontist's chair at ten years old with tears running down my cheeks, powerless to tell him he had not used nearly enough novocaine. I can still feel the burning pain of a knife scraping my soft palate.

Then there was the embarrassment that followed, as I had to sit in the principal's office during recess. For one week, while my mouth healed, I was not to run, jump, or play in the schoolyard. Not that I enjoyed doing any of these things, mind you. But during recess, the only place where I could be supervised besides the schoolyard was the office, which was the same place you had to go if you were in trouble and banned from recess. I hated that everyone thought I was in trouble all week, even though, in hindsight, I'm sure no one even noticed.

Also, there was The Sneeze. About five days post-op, one fateful night, my parents left me and my siblings home alone. It happened when I was playing Barbies in my room. (Yes, I played Barbies at ten years old and I would still play with them now if they weren't way up in my dad's garage, and if I had the time, and, no, I didn't reveal this to Dan until after we got married. I am immature, not stupid.) I sneezed, which apparently loosened my stitches, and blood gushed from my mouth. I urged my older brother to call 911, which he did not do. Instead, a neighbor was summoned and we applied a cold washcloth to my mouth, which stopped the bleeding for the most part. The next morning I took a trip to Nastytown when I vomited blood.

OK, so now it's twenty-three years later, I am due for another round of this fun-ness, and I'm breastfeeding, which means I don't get to have the fun drugs (Halcyon—I'm not really sure what it is, but I am sure I would love it) during the procedure. Percoset is also incompatible with breastfeeding. Or maybe it would help with sleep training…(KIDDING!!). So I'm going into my graft with nothing but the promise of novocaine (hopefully enough this time) and Advil, and I'm a bit nervous. So I had an unmedicated birth. Big deal. Childbirth is normal and natural. Having someone scrape out part of your mouth with a scalpel and sew it onto another part of your mouth isn't.

But then I got to my periodontist's office. I was greeted by a blast of crisp air-conditioning and a smile at the front desk. I was welcomed to a beverage from the mini-fridge (don't mind if I do) and offered a magazine (*Runner's World*, thank you) while I waited. Then it was time to head back to the chair. The assistant, who I would totally be friends with in real life, chatted with me and offered me a blanket (yes, please) and headphones (no, thanks). Then they turned on the back massaging dental chair. It was just as nice as anything you would find at Brookstone. They numbed me up so good, I could barely feel it when they inserted the sharp instruments. I shut my eyes and focused on remaining calm. Dare I say, the whole experience was…relaxing?

When I got home, I took a few Advil and waited for the anesthesia to wear off and for the real pain to begin. But it never did. Meanwhile, my mother-in-law had insisted on coming over to help with Sweet Pea so I could have some time to recover. She shooed me into my bedroom, adamant that I rest while she tend to the baby, so I had no choice but to lie in bed. I tried sleeping but couldn't, so I read and caught up a little on Twitter. This was no post-operative haze; it was more like a spa vacation. Or at least a relaxing morning at home with childcare.

I just finished a bowl of Häagen-Dazs because I am only supposed to eat soft foods for a week. Now, I've worked with chronically ill people and I know how annoying it is when people use their sickness to their advantage… But I kinda get why they do it.

50

Notes from a Terminal Night Person

SOME PEOPLE ARE morning people. You know who you are. You wake up with a smile on your face like it's totally normal to be up before the sun. At an hour when the songbirds are just beginning to warm up, you are glad to be alive, grateful to be present for yet another glorious day. And just like you wake up ready to face the world with nary a cup of coffee, you shut down just as quickly.

Have you ever seen a morning person at night? They are easily mistaken for a drunk person, the way they go from completely alert and animated to passed out in a matter of mere seconds. Perhaps it's only natural that they shut down so forcefully, considering they've been completely awake since practically the day before.

Night people, on the other hand, discover that things are just getting good around 10 p.m. When everyone else is sleeping, night owls are the most creative, productive…dare I say, brilliant? Morning people might guffaw at this proclamation, but how would they know what's going on when they are fast asleep, oblivious.

But I confess: I've always wanted to be a morning person. I'd love to know what it's like to wake up feeling rested and alert. I envy those who can put an early morning workout on their calendar and know that it's definitely going to happen. The idea of leisurely sipping coffee from my favorite ceramic mug with plenty of time, instead of rushing around to find the lid to the travel mug two seconds before I absolutely need to leave, is heavenly. But it's just not how I'm made. Believe me, I've tried. If living with a six-month-old human alarm clock that goes off daily between 4:30 and 6:30 hasn't made a morning person out of me yet, I don't know what will.

Are you a night person too? If you are unsure, here are some guidelines that may help you decide.

You May Be A Night Person If

- You take at least an hour to wind down before shutting off the light. Your winding-down ritual may include checking email, going through the Valpak coupons, setting up your French press for the next morning, laying out tomorrow's outfit, checking email again, loading the dishwasher, taking out your contacts, brushing your teeth, checking email again, giving the bathroom sink a wipe, and reading a chapter of your book.
- You congratulate yourself all day long for waking up anytime before 7 a.m.
- Your first thought upon waking is *SNOOZE BUTTON*.
- Going to bed anytime before 10:30 is a huge deal, generally reserved only for special occasions, such as any night during the last trimester of pregnancy.
- You secretly think getting tired anytime before 11 is a sign of weakness.
- You think one of the best things about being an adult is setting your own bedtime.

51
If It Looks Like a Duck, Swims Like a Duck, and Quacks Like a Duck… Then It's Probably a Duck (Where Duck = Voicemail)

TODAY I CHECKED the voicemail on my land line. This hardly seems worth writing about, except that it was the first time I'd checked the messages on my land line—ever. And by ever, I mean never before. As in Comcast connected our phone service a year ago and up to today I had not once, ever, checked the voicemail that apparently was part of our service package (who knew?).

Ever since we got the phone, I thought it was odd that in the display window of the phone, there was an icon of an envelope and it said New Voicemail. I assumed this was some sort of default setting. My goal was to pay as little as possible for the phone service. We already had an answering machine, so there was no need for bells and whistles, like voicemail.

Also, there was this annoying tone instead of a dial tone. I've used voicemail systems before and it sounded just like the tone that indicates messages are waiting. But we couldn't possibly have messages waiting if we didn't have voicemail, I told myself. I was sure it was some kind of glitch. A very annoying glitch, but nothing with which to concern myself.

Then there was the pesky issue of people telling me they'd left me messages I'd never received. I could only assume these people were full of crap or that they had left messages on my cell and somehow Verizon Wireless ate the messages before I could listen to them. Because Verizon totally does that… Right?

And all the people who were supposed to call me back but, according to me, never did? Luckily, my gargantuan ego prevented my feelings from becoming hurt over these slights. Thankfully, all friendships have come through this voicemail problem intact, as my reactions to unreturned phone calls ranged from indifference/ignorance to mild surprise.

Finally I opened my eyes to the fact that all the signs pointing to a year's worth of ignored voicemails were indeed adding up to the simple truth: There was actually a year's worth of ignored voicemails on my phone. Once I called Comcast and cleared things up, I had the pleasure of experiencing at least a dozen epiphanies, all within the time it takes to listen to dozens of new messages. It was almost worth it just for the joy of all the aha moments that just kept coming, one after another, fast and furious.

I learned that my BFF is something of a phone stalker because half the messages were from her, and yet I never felt neglected by her, not once, ever, as she had the good sense to leave messages on both my land line and my cell.

I discovered my optometrist wasn't a lazy slob like I'd thought. He had indeed called to say my glasses were ready last

January. Same thing with my eye doctor's office—it turned out they did call to say my contacts were ready for pickup in February.

I found out six months too late that one of my girlfriends really couldn't say when she could get together that week because her husband hadn't gotten his work schedule yet. In February, another girlfriend was just so happy that we'd had a healthy baby and was excited to stop by and see us. In July, the girl who would later become one of our favorite babysitters called to say she was sad that she wouldn't be able to do Fridays (good thing I persisted despite her supposed failure to return my call). Last month, our cleaning lady was sorry she'd accidentally broken a glass.

I guess the lesson here is just if it looks like voicemail and it acts like voicemail, it's probably voicemail. And I suppose the other lesson is don't hold a grudge when people don't call you back. Not that I held a grudge; as I said, I barely noticed. I'm just saying I would have had a lot of explaining to do if I had been a grudge holder in this case.

52

The Unofficial YAY! List of Cool Things about a Five-Hour Flight Delay with a Baby

I'M TIRED OF hearing about how hard life with a baby is. Yes, of course it's hard, but it's also awesome, and people need to not be inundated with horror stories about all the ways in which your life will change once you have a baby, because this may cause pregnant women undue stress and vivid nightmares (hypothetically, of course), which is just not worth it.

I just needed to get that complaint out of my system while I still can because my New Year's Resolution 2013 #1a is Complain Less. This is a corollary to resolution #1, Be More Grateful. In the spirit of my intentions for the new year, I bring you The Unofficial YAY! List of Cool Things about a Five-Hour Flight Delay with a Baby.

We had an 8:25 a.m. flight from Providence to Denver, which meant a wake-up call of 5:30 a.m. Yuck. Have I mentioned I'm not a morning person? I hit refresh on the Southwest app on my phone, under the warm cozy covers, hopeful that there was a delay that would justify hitting the snooze button another time or two, to no avail. As it turned out, I could have hit the snooze button about forty-five times and still made the flight, but we didn't know this until 9:30, at which point we'd been sitting on the plane on the tarmac for more than an hour... We were informed there was a safety issue and that we would be leaving at 1:10 p.m. Which turned out to be 1:35, but whatever.

Because we didn't pack a lunch, we ate at an airport restaurant. I should have known my glass of sauvignon blanc would be ridiculously expensive, considering a) it was purchased at an airport, and b) the menu did not list the prices. However, it wasn't until we got the bill that we realized it was a $13 glass of wine. For the record, I don't buy bottles of wine that cost more than $12.99. Anyway, not knowing what a rip-off the wine was, I savored it happily.

YAY #1: ENJOYED STUPIDLY EXPENSIVE GLASS OF WINE

WHILE DRINKING SAID glass of wine and eating lunch, we discovered how much Sweet Pea enjoyed oyster crackers. They were complimentary, which makes me feel better about the wine. You know what I liked better than watching my daughter feast on her new treat? Scooping her out of her high chair and finding 80 percent of the crushed crackers on the floor and knowing someone else was going to clean them up. Maybe the glass of wine was a bargain after all.

YAY #2: NO CLEANING UP THE HIGH CHAIR OR THE KITCHEN FLOOR

NOT REALIZING WE were embarking on what would become a twelve-hour journey, we packed neither lunch nor an adequate diaper supply. The night before our trip, three disposable diapers seemed like plenty. But by the time we lined up for family boarding (for the second time) with one lonely diaper in the diaper bag,

I feared our rations were insufficient. I saw a lady with a slightly older baby and asked if she had extra diapers. She said she did, although they were a size too big. A roomy diaper would be better than no diaper so I thanked her for whatever she could spare. Before the handoff was complete, the Diaper Fairy appeared in the form of a bearded stranger who happened to overhear us. He came bearing two size 2s and to him we are so grateful. This small act of kindness reinforced my faith in humanity.

YAY #3: Visit from Diaper Fairy

As far as what we did for four hours at the airport… There was a lot of walking with Sweet Pea in the Ergo Carrier in an attempt to get her to sleep. Which was successful, though it resulted in a sore back for me… It was totally worth it, however, because sleep she did. I even successfully performed the Superstealth Ergo Carrier to Airport Floor Maneuver, which resulted in thirty minutes of sweet toddler sleep (on the floor).

YAY #4: Baby napped on airport floor

But you know what else we did? Dan worked while I followed Sweet Pea around as she explored the gate area. Believe me, I had reservations about letting her crawl around the T.F. Green Airport floor. But the alternative was holding her captive in the stroller or in my lap, neither of which seemed a) pleasant for her, b) pleasant for me, or c) conducive to getting her to take her afternoon nap in flight. P.S. Did you know the best way to get a long flight with a baby to seem shorter, besides reading a great book (which actually isn't possible when you have a baby on your lap, that is, unless you like reading a sentence every two minutes and testing your reflexes to make sure pages aren't gleefully ripped from your book), is for the baby to nap. Much like the rest interval during a hard workout, time passes faster when a baby is asleep. That must defy some law of physics, but I swear to god it's true.

Oh yeah, so the good part of all this letting Sweet Pea crawl around the disgusting germ-filled airport floor—it helped me to be less hyper about germs. When strangers got all up in her grill, instead of bracing myself for the uncomfortable moment when they would put their hand on her hand or, worse yet, on her chubby cheek, I was like *Whatever, bring it on. Nothing on your hand could possibly be worse than whatever is on the floor she was just practically licking.* And we all survived.

YAY #5: G*ERMS NOT AS BIG OF A DEAL AS PREVIOUSLY FEARED*

A*LSO*—SWEET PEA WAS just as happy to crawl aimlessly, stopping only to be admired by strangers, or to gawk at older, more mobile children as she was strewing her toys and the contents of every low drawer about our house, and there was nothing for me to clean up. I'm not saying that made it worth it, but then again, how often does your baby make a mess that you don't have to clean up?

YAY #6: N*O CLEANING UP THE PLAY AREA*

OH, AND WE scored four hundred dollars worth of vouchers for our next Southwest trip. I think I would still rather have had the flight leave on time, but it's better than a stick in the eye. And btw, I've had a stick in the eye. They have to measure my corneal pressure every time I go to the eye doctor, so I know what I'm talking about.

YAY #7: MONEY

SO DON'T WORRY about air travel with a little one. As long as you don't lose the baby in the airport, it will probably be fine.

53

What If They Say My Duck Is Wet Because It's Wet?

I'VE BEEN THINKING about an offhand comment my cousin made about my blog. I don't get to see this cousin as often as I'd like due to geographical issues. She checks up on me via my ramblings on Whatevs…which I love. Having never been to any meeting that ends in the word *anonymous*, I can only imagine a blogger's thirst for readership being akin to a junkie's obsession with just one more hit.

While I love to know anyone reads my blog, and all the information presented there is true, I need to clear something up. It is not my diary. It's more like a reality show where I am the star, the producer, the cinematographer, and the film editor (minus anyone killing or voting anyone off). It's about me, and I don't make anything up. But I choose the angles and the lighting. I pluck out the good scenes and leave 99.99 percent of the footage on the cutting room floor. Yeah, I know some bloggers put it all out there and that's what draws big-time readership and comments by the bucketload. But I'm not a famous blogger. I have a regular job and someday I might need another regular job and a potential employer will google me, and after they've seen pictures of my hoo-ha while giving birth, will they think I am the most professional candidate? Doubtful. And that is the reason (actually, among many others, which we don't need to get into) why I'm not sharing hoo-ha pictures. (Actually I don't have any.) That said, I do look pretty happy, rosy cheeked, and alert in the birth photos. Well, the ones after the baby was born, anyway. That's what having no medication on board will do for you.

So, back to my original point, which is, if you're still following—I swear I'm coming around to it—I totally have problems! I just don't necessarily write about them. Not, like, crazy interesting problems, like issues with substance abuse (unless Cool Whip is a substance). I am not estranged from anyone in my family, and I don't have an eating disorder (unless you count problems with the aforementioned Cool Whip). I'm just a normal person, and despite my New Year's Resolution to be more grateful, I have my stuff.

Like, I can be really high-strung and obsessive about certain things, and I can't deal with those things without talking them through. Earlier today I was informed that I rubbed someone the wrong way at work. I found out thirdhand that someone in another department felt we had a "negative interaction." Upon hearing this, I felt awful. Was I rude without even realizing it? Does this person hate me? How will I deal with the mortification of having to deal with this person professionally in the future?

Perhaps a normal grown-up would just deal with these feelings and move on. Not me. I Gchatted my best friend in a frenzy. "Are you there? I'm so embarrassed!" She didn't reply. A normal grown-up would have assumed she was busy working as this was during typical work hours. Yeah, not me. I texted her frantically, "Can you talk!?" Thankfully, she could. She talked me down. We made a plan. Next time I see the jilted person, I will apologize for having been abrupt. (I honestly don't remember everything about the interaction, but I guess if she thinks it was a negative interaction I ought to apologize.)

Or take the Listen To Your Mother show I am working on. I am pretty jazzed about it, but there are many moving pieces and many questions that come up with each new task. Poor Dan. He gets to hear me obsess every night. *Should I call or email? Email. Definitely email, then follow up with a phone call. No…call, then follow up with an email. For sure, call then email. What do you think? Hey, can you read this email before I hit send? Does that sound good? Does that make sense? Should I copy and paste the text into an email or send it as an attachment?…Helvetica or Times New Roman?* OK, I don't really ask him about the font, but I'm sure it feels that way to him sometimes.

Sometimes when I get crazy, I think of my niece. Well, she's not really my niece. She's my cousin's fiancé's daughter. Not the cousin I mentioned earlier, a different one. Dan thinks I think the whole world is my cousin. I don't. I just have a lot of extended family. And I thought it would be easier to just call her my niece.

She's three and she's a sweet, earnest, adorable kid. And you might say she's a little anxious. I heard tell of a conversation that went down in the car en route to my brother and sister-in-law's house, where she was going to be with my (actual) niece and nephew and their babysitter for the evening. Little Emma (not her real name) asked questions the whole ride there, holding her duck close. Her stuffed animal/washcloth duck is her security blanket. She takes it everywhere and sucks on it for comfort. "What if the new babysitter won't let me suck my duck?" She would. "What if I suck my duck?" Then you will. And my personal favorite: "What if they say my duck is wet because it's wet?" When I heard that, I laughed, and I thought *Emma, I feel you.*

Lately I've been thinking of that. It makes me smile to myself and it also reminds me not to be a three-year-old. So my new mantra is "What if they say my duck is wet because it's wet?" Don't say I don't have problems.

54

True Story: I Met My Husband at a Bar

ON VALENTINE'S DAY, years ago, I lived with two roommates I found on Craigslist. I had packed my Jetta and driven cross-country, alone, except for the company of my GPS, just two weeks prior. I was thousands of miles from home. I had no job, no man, and practically no friends in Boulder. I was quite the catch.

My roommates invited me out to a bar for an Anti-Valentine's Day Party. I had nothing else going on, and I was on the prowl, so I happily agreed. As we stepped out of the car, my roommate asked me, "What is your intention for the night?" I looked at her like she was nuts. She wasn't nuts, she was just into Landmark and creating her own future and stuff like that. I didn't want to jinx anything, but she said that's not how it works, you have to say your intention out loud. So I said I was looking for true love. I'd loved boyfriends in the past, but I was twenty-nine years old and I had never actually been *in love*, not one single time, and I was beginning to think I was a total freak.

After having a couple of drinks at the bar, I noticed a Semitic-looking guy a few tables over and decided to talk to him. Not because I was so interested in him as a male specimen, but more because I felt compelled to find out if there were any Jews besides me in the Wild West. But once I sat down and started talking to the guy who would indeed turn out to be a fellow Hebe, I noticed his cute friend. The cute friend and I got to talking. I told him I didn't really know anyone in town but I would soon, and I love to set people up, so I needed to know his vital stats… He told me he was thirty-one and a self-employed software developer (so far so good). I asked him what his type was. After a thoughtful pause, he replied, "Smart, kind, loves the outdoors…and beautiful." So I told him, "I have an idea! You should call me."

We hung out for the rest of the night, talking and dancing (side note: he tricked me into thinking he liked dancing!). The minute I woke up the next morning, I frantically called my sister because I COULD NOT WAIT ANOTHER MINUTE for Dan to get in touch. My sister reminded me it had been less than eight hours since I'd last seen him and I needed to take it easy. But at 1:10, there was a text from him saying "Good luck." He'd remembered I had a 1:30 job interview.

Two Februarys later, we closed on our house. And two Februarys after that, we became a family.

Happy Valentine's Day!

55

Home Alone

LAST WEEKEND, I came home from my run to find my house looking like a drunk midget had burglarized it. I'm used to this, as I live with a thirteen-month-old who is into everything within her wingspan. I called out to see where everyone was and got no response. I peeked into the bedrooms. No one. I stuck my head down the stairwell to the basement. I heard no activity. I looked out the window and saw no one in the backyard. *I was home alone.* The last time I could remember feeling as ecstatic about this circumstance as I did at that moment had to have been in 1996 when my parents dropped my little sister at a friend's house and left town for two nights.

What would I do with myself!? I was so excited I could hardly think straight. Every possibility crammed itself into my mind at once… COFFEE! SHOWER! LAUNDRY! READ! BLOG! ORGANIZE CLOSET! WATCH *GIRLS*!

I decided the shower would be a waste of time because that's freebie alone time, even if anyone else is home. Except on the days when Sweet Pea insists on playing peekaboo with me through the shower curtain, of course. Coffee could be consumed while engaging in any other task and would intensify my enjoyment of whatever it was I would ultimately choose, so I started boiling water for the French press. I found the Styles section of the *New York Times* and settled down on the couch, but before I could even flip to Modern Love, I heard the sound of the key in the lock, looked up, and there in the front doorway stood Dan and Sweet Pea. Cue the sad trombone "Wah wah wah wah" sound.

Dan must have been paying close attention because this Saturday he asked, "Would you like me to take Sweet Pea out for a walk so you can have some alone time at home?" *You bet your ass I would.* And there I sat… Coffee in hand, laptop on lap, documenting that moment for posterity.

Who'd have thunk being home alone at thirty-four would feel as good as or, dare I say, better than it did when I was twelve?

56

There's No Room for Fear in a Burley Trailer

I THOUGHT I had put my fear of road biking behind me. My longtime readers (hi, Mom!) may be sitting here like, *What you talkin' bout, Willis?* but there was a time, long ago, when I was terrified of riding my bike anywhere near cars. So, early in my cycling career I became a bike slut. I was willing to ride with literally anyone until I was comfortable enough to ride solo with car traffic. I had one riding partner whom I'm ashamed to admit to even knowing; he was about my dad's age at the time, and he was fond of bashing his wife and kids on our rides. One night, he invited me to his house for dinner after a ride. At the time it seemed weird, but not too weird to accept the free meal. But thinking about it now, I cringe at the inappropriateness of it. I wonder what I was thinking, but knowing me, I was probably afraid I would hurt his feelings if I declined. Never mind the fact I could hardly stand him. I can only imagine what his wife thought when her husband unexpectedly brought a spandex-clad twenty-four-year-old female cycling buddy home to the family dinner she'd prepared. Fast forward ten years. I've biked Mount Evans, East Portal Road near Black Canyon of the Gunnison, all around Arizona, and all kinds of other badass stuff. Yet, after all this time I'm still way too concerned about what other people think of me. And I'm still having issues with fear around road biking. Because now, attached to the same Specialized Allez I bought with my 2003 tax return and some help from my parents all those years ago is a Burley trailer with my beating heart sitting inside, wearing a teeny tiny monkey-print helmet.

I used to think it wasn't worth my time to change, pump up my tires, and ride if I wasn't going *at least* fifteen to twenty miles. On Thursday, I spent no less than fifty-five minutes figuring out how to connect the Burley to the bike, adjusting Sweet Pea's brand-new helmet, pumping up my tires, pumping up the Burley tires, attaching the flag to the Burley, intermittently taking sticks and stones out of Sweet Pea's mouth and sprinting to snatch her up before she crawled into the street while I was attending to these tasks, and by the time we were ready to go, naptime was hovering close like a supervisor with stale breath, and I still hadn't fed her lunch. But hell if I wasn't going to take us for a spin after all that effort. So we went around the block twice, and I considered it an excellent use of my time, since it meant The First Time was now out of the way.

Today, library story hour was scheduled for 10:15, and the sun was shining. At 8:05 I Skype messaged Dan, "I want to bike down to the Main Branch with Sweet Pea in the Burley but I'm scared." I don't know if I was hoping he'd hold me, send an escort, or what, but he encouraged me to go and sent me a link to a Google Map with a route to the library that would keep us exclusively on bike paths. After a mere twenty minutes of prep (Rome wasn't built in a day, people), I pretended I knew what I was doing, and off we went.

I really hope Sweet Pea bought it because it is my understanding that a) children smell fear, and b) kids can never know parents are scared because that is just, like, against the order of the entire universe. I think we're cool because she slept the whole time.

The ride was uneventful. Save for getting a little turned around (I'm still just as bad with directions as I ever was) and discovering parts of the CU campus I never knew about, everything went as planned. And I felt like a beast climbing up University Hill towing an extra forty-seven pounds of trailer and child.

If the last ten years have taught me anything, it's to deal with fear by just doing whatever I'm scared of (sans creepy, older, married men).

57

A Day in the Life

5:35 Awaken to the faint sound of "eh-eh-eh." hope it will go away. "Eh-eh-eh" escalates to full-blown crying.

5:38 Nurse baby. Consider staying awake after nursing to run. Reject ridiculous idea.

5:55 Put baby and self back to sleep.

6:55 Baby crying. Husband says he will check diaper.

6:56 Wonder why husband is taking so long.

7:30 Tiptoe to bathroom in hopes of using it alone. Feel smug once in bathroom with door shut.

7:44 Feel excited and grateful for coffee.

7:46 Meal time. Baby throws thinly sliced banana slices on floor. Baby throws lovingly cut cubes of kiwi on floor. Baby throws avocado pieces on floor.

7:52 Remember mantra: *Don't react*. Remind yourself you are awesome parent for not making food into power struggle.

8:00 Consider getting dressed. Microwave coffee again. Need to check email first. And Facebook. And make a few phone calls.

9:06   After getting dressed, realize your outfit kind of matches the baby's outfit. Do not consider changing anyone's outfit.

9:30   Attach Burley trailer to bike, collect helmets, lock, backpack with one eye on baby, hoping she doesn't crawl into street/eat rocks, sticks, grass, et al.

10:30   Arrive at library story hour fifteen minutes late per usual. Watch baby walk around, get up in other people's faces/laps/business/sippy cups/crumbs/food pouches. Remember mantra: *If no one is crying do not intervene.* Remind yourself you are awesome free-range parent. Catch up on Google Reader while intermittently looking up to supervise baby.

11:45   Meal time. See above. (Turkey, bread, and cheese on floor this time.)

12:10   Put baby down for nap.

12:15   Open computer to start blog post. First must check email. And Facebook. Remember to feed chickens. Make necessary phone calls. Fold laundry. Pay bills.

2:35   Remotivate to write blog post.

2:38   Hear baby crying. Warm up a sippy cup of milk and retrieve crying baby.

3:00   Feel too tired to do anything but lie on living room floor. Invite baby to cuddle. Remind baby it is OK to touch near belly button but not OK to poke belly button. After second belly button poke, tuck shirt in and limit access to belly button.

5:45   Call husband. Casually ask when he will be home from work. Just curious…

6:00   Feed baby dinner. See "Meal Time" as above. (Chicken, avocado, tortilla on floor this time.)

7:00   Baby asleep. At least in crib with light off.

7:10   Start blog post again.

8:30 Hit Publish.
9:30 Husband says he is going to bed. Tell him will be right there.
10:10 Get in bed.

58

What's the Deal with Park Etiquette?

WHAT'S THE DEAL with park etiquette? I am familiar with gym etiquette, road cycling etiquette, wedding etiquette, and driving etiquette. Though I am not saying I necessarily follow the driving etiquette. I'm a Rhode Island-ah, after all. But parent-child social interaction is largely virgin territory for me. I'm not talking about the stuff you're thinking of... A simple Google search of "park etiquette parents" turned up the obvious pointers, like supervise your child, don't bring a sick kid to the park, and be respectful.

I'm wondering how friendly or unfriendly you are supposed to be with the other parents/caregivers... Because yesterday, it was all awkward starfish at the neighborhood park.

It started out normal. We rolled up and upon sweet exile from her stroller, Sweet Pea was all about the gravel. The climbing structures, the swings, the miniature house? Not even on her radar. As far as Sweet Pea was concerned, we were at an All-You-Can-Eat Gravel Buffet. She was hitting the gravel hard and going back for seconds, thirds, and fourths, oblivious to my repeated imperative, "Not in your mouth!"

And then she caught sight of the other kid and the gravel was nothing more than a distant memory. She ambled up the concrete stairs with laser-sharp focus, her eyes on the little girl with the bear hat, yelling "Ha! Ha! Haey! Hi! Hi!" until she caught the girl's attention. Their eyes locked. From a distance of eight feet, with only the plastic walls of a miniature house between them, they were caught in each other's gaze, Sweet Pea grinning her (mostly) toothless grin while the little girl stood silently with a shy smile.

I smiled, first at the child, and then at the adult companion (presumably the mother). But she wouldn't make eye contact. I said hi. She did not engage. Now, I'm not looking for a new best friend. Or even a park buddy. Or anything, really. Seriously, not even a babysitter or a tax accountant. I'm good with all that. But what do you do when your child is engaged in a staring contest to end all staring contests and she's too little and too unsteady to be so close to concrete stairs for you to walk away and the parent of the other child won't acknowledge your existence with even the vaguest hint of a nod?

Believe me, I get wanting to let your child roam free in a safe area while you catch up on email, Google Reader, Twitter, and/or Facebook. I mean, in the theoretical sense, of course, I can understand why one might do this. Not that I have ever gone to the library for exactly this purpose. And not that I'm annoyed that I can't do this anymore because Sweet Pea has discovered the joy of walking around all areas of the library with a piece of chalk that she either has in her mouth or dangerously close to the pages of the books.

But this woman wasn't letting her kid roam free. In fact, the kid fell sort of on her face (from a height of about eighteen inches) at one point and appeared to be 100 percent fine, and the mom made this huge deal out of it. Admittedly, for all I know the kid has issues that I don't presume to understand and it would actually be a huge deal if she fell on her face, so I am not judging. I'm just saying, the mom was less zoning out and more swooping in.

So she wasn't there to let her kid run free while she chillaxed, and she wasn't there to make friends. But even a half nod could have conveyed so much. In her eyes I might have understood *I am so over this miniature house. I sit in here for, like, five hours a week. I'm tired, my house is a mess, and I don't have the energy for a full nod or even a hello, but I know you feel me, sister.* I totally would have gotten that.

Instead, I was left to wonder how long we were going to act like the other didn't exist (indefinitely, it turned out) and whether I was being way too sensitive (probably, yes), and if there is some unwritten code of Park Etiquette. And if there is, can you fill a mother in? Thanks.

59

Getting Back to My Roots: A Tale of Triumph in the Face of Adversity

I'M NOT VERY good at working from home. I don't mean the mom gig, because that just happens at home. And the park. And the library. And on the damp floor of the rec center locker room, cold, wet, and naked. But I digress.

What you might not imagine is how hard it is for me to let Dan work from home. To give you an idea of just how hard it is for me to avoid asking him one little question, checking with him about one little date on the calendar, or inquiring—just real quick—about the whereabouts of just one missing item, I will sum it up thusly: Even if he works on the weekend, he goes into the office.

And this makes me mad. Not that it has much (if anything) to do with me, but that's just how I roll. "It's all about Pam," sung in a singsong voice, is a much repeated phrase in our house. And it's not me, Sweet Pea, or the chickens repeating it. Seriously, though, if Dan is working during a time when Sweet Pea is sleeping, I might like to go somewhere. My absence would not impact his ability to work, and his presence ensures that our sleeping child is safe. Which would be a win-win. Except, if I can't leave him alone when I am there, he can't concentrate on work.

Which brings us to Sunday night. I set out to do just that—leave him the hell alone. Because he was working from home, and I needed to prove to him that I could let him. The challenges were great and they were many. Because Sunday was the day we got me a power trimmer/edger. See, "we" bought it from our shared bank account, but I'm the only one who is going to use it, considering I'm the only one who cares whether our lawn looks nice, and up till Sunday our backyard kind of looked like a junkyard. Piles of hoses littered one corner, black trash bags of leaves occupied another, against the house lay a forlorn twelve-foot ladder, and by the back door sat a cracked, faded Rubbermaid tub full of chicken feed. Dandelions poked through the ground on our flagstone patio. And some random logs were stacked in no particular order along the side fence. If our chickens could talk, they would probably want to renegotiate the terms of their lease.

I've been wanting to do something about the state of the yard for a long time, but there never seemed to be time. On Sunday, the stars had finally aligned. Here was a weekend day that was neither too warm nor too cold. I wasn't working. Dan was available and willing to help me with the yard. Sweet Pea took a three-hour nap. In those three hours, I accomplished more than I've ever accomplished in that yard over the three years we've lived in this house.

I moved stuff into the garage, created a to-donate pile, trashed what Dan confirmed was actually trash (apparently looking like trash does not necessarily qualify an item as trash), and tossed compostables in the compost. When that was done, I mowed, weeded, transplanted, mulched, and watered like a crazed gardening maniac.

When the sun had set, the baby was put to bed, and Dan descended into the basement to work, my real challenge began: Operation Do Not Disturb Working Husband. And yet it was at this moment that I embarked on another challenge: Assemble New Power Tool. I futzed. I finagled. I shoved. I yanked. I teetered on the edge of nail breakage. With the baby sleeping in the next room, I avoided cursing (loudly). With my husband working in the basement, I came dangerously—I mean like "bringing three children under the age of five to the edge of the Grand Canyon and not holding their hands and letting them throw rocks" (yes, I actually witnessed this)—close to bothering him, seeking his expert counsel on how best to deal with the rogue part that I couldn't slide onto the thingy, even though I was doing everything just like the picture in the user manual showed. And also, the battery pack. Why wouldn't it slide onto the battery pack holder? I had so many questions. And the one person I knew could answer all of them was a mere holler away, yet trying to work.

So I did what I used to do before I met Dan all those years ago. No, not daydream about how I was going to meet someone smart, sexy, and Jewish named Mark on a plane and it would be this unbelievable coincidence that we lived on the same block and were obviously soul mates and had, like, everything in common, including a shared love of road biking, *Sex and the City*, and Barbara's Shredded Oats cereal and were somehow only just now meeting on a plane, which was extra random since it was Southwest and so *seats weren't even assigned*. Not that. I mean, I did it myself. I solved the mysteries of the Black & Decker assembly instructions.

When Dan came up the stairs, I beamed, triumphant in all my Trimmer and Edger Assembling Glory and told him, "While you were working, I totally figured out the new tool. I'm, like, getting back to my roots."

He looked at me with a sly smile. "You mean you called your dad?"

"What-EVER!"

It's hard for me to come up with anything clever to say under pressure. And besides, his comment was completely out of line and unfair. I would *never* have called my dad for something like this. I'm not sure if I've ever even seen him change a lightbulb.

I would have called my mom, obviously.

60

Home Is Where the Mom Is

I STEPPED OUT from the car onto the pavement of the Departures area and peeked at Sweet Pea, who was content to play with her bee toy in her carseat. Then I hauled my mom's orange suitcase out of the trunk and turned to hug her. As soon as my face met the fabric of her shirt, the tears started to flow.

"I hate it when you leave." My words were muffled as I buried my wet face into her neck and shoulder, but she got the idea.

"But we will get to see each other again soon."

This was true. We have a wedding come up. And then I go back to Rhode Island for a long visit this summer. This takes away some of the sting.

You might think it gets a little easier, but I cry every time my mom and I part ways at an airport. It doesn't matter which of us is the one who leaves. It's just as likely to happen at T.F. Green as it is at Denver International.

You might assume I get weepy because I am overwhelmed, wondering who is going to whip up lunches for Sweet Pea, easily mend the J.Crew skirt I got at Goodwill for $3.50, or organize my

Tupperware cabinet once she's left. And maybe that's part of it. Who doesn't treasure the capable and willing hands of a mother?

But it's more than that. It's the momness of her—that makes you feel safe, loved, and at home. Not that home isn't the place where the mail piles up, the basement floods once in a while, and you sometimes forget to dump a poopy diaper into the toilet and you walk in the nursery an hour later and you're like, "Oh my god, what stinks?" Home is definitely that place.

Home is also the place where spontaneous dancing in the kitchen occurs (sometimes with the baby, sometimes without). It's where a vase full of flowers picked from the front yard by Dan and Sweet Pea might greet you when you walk in the door after work.

But home isn't just a place. It's also the feeling I get when I'm with my mom. And the older I get the more I realize I don't think I'm going to outgrow it.

61

Fat Talk: I'm Totally Quitting...Tomorrow

"Dude, my butt looks so big in this suit."

"No, man, your butt is awesome. Girls like a man with some junk in the trunk. Check out my hair, though. It's thinning and I can't do anything with it. Should I wear a hat or just shave what's left of it?"

"You have plenty of hair. Have you seen my crow's-feet!?"

Said no men, ever.

So why do women talk like this all the time? You had to have seen the fat talk clip from the *Today* show. I even saw it and I don't have a TV.

The experts on the *Today* show run through a litany of reasons why women commiserate about how fat/unattractive we are. I agree with everything they said—especially that little part they mention right at the end: Body bashing perpetuates poor self-esteem and **you should never do it in front of your kids**.

No duh, right? Before I had Sweet Pea, I promised myself and Dan that I would never do this once our baby was born, *especially* if we had a girl. Never again would I say any of the following:

I feel so fat right now.
Does this outfit make me look huge?
I just ate so much cake. I'm gross.
Is my stomach sticking out?
I didn't used to have cellulite. Here, see? Look at the cellulite.
   LOOK AT IT.

It would be like a fat talk fast…forever. It would be good for me. I was actually looking forward to it. Kind of like how I look forward to the 5:30 a.m. workouts; they're so good in theory, yet so rarely executed.

I went to a really interesting talk on neurolinguistics last spring where I learned that you can influence your thoughts and feelings based on the words you use, both in your communication with others and in your self-talk. I know this has been true for me with sports. Some of my best times have been recorded when my body was ready to quit while my mind said "Yes, I can, yes, I can." (This turned out to be a good strategy for enduring natural childbirth too).

You might be surprised at how easily I can tell myself "Yes, I can" when in fact I feel like I absolutely can't, given the fact that I can hardly breathe and my legs are on fire. I do it because it's what I've always done. I do it because I work so hard at moving toward my athletic goals, it would be a waste not to give myself the free speed that comes with a good attitude. I do it because I know how good it feels to see a faster time on the finish clock. I do it because I know how easy it is to back off and how quickly you go from backing off to giving up once your mind goes to "No, I can't."

So why can't I give the same positive attitude and discipline into avoiding fat talk, especially around my child? Oh, yeah—all those resolutions I had about ending it just as soon as I gave birth—just add them to the growing list of stuff I said I'd never do once I had a kid, but still do.

So I make excuses. *Sweet Pea is only fifteen months old. She doesn't understand what I'm saying. Even if she understands, she can't talk yet, so I have a few months till I really have to quit. I'll quit soon. Anyway, I always tell her I love her little body. I find her chubby tummy especially delicious and she knows that. And her pudgy thighs! I adore the thighs. She'll be fine. She's not really watching me.*

Except, I know that's not true. When she was a few weeks old, I would lay her down on her back on the bathroom floor while I scrunched some product in my hair and applied my makeup. I'd glance down intermittently and catch sight of her eyes darting around, following my every move. Lately, she has started to root around in my clutch whenever I go to pay for something. She's not just exploring, she's going straight for my lip balm and she doesn't stop until she gets it into her little hands and "applies" it to her lips. (Her inability to unscrew the cap is a minor detail.) And I know she's been watching me when she goes to the closet and grabs the broom and the dustpan and drags them around the house. (If she were really paying attention, she'd be focusing on the two-foot radius surrounding her high chair, however.)

She's got her eyes on me. And I'm still making disparaging statements about my body, albeit not as often as I used to. Though I would be lying if I said that was because my self-awareness and body acceptance have blossomed since I stepped into motherhood. (Or since motherhood trampled me; how I look at it depends on when you ask me.) It's probably because I weigh less than I've ever weighed as an adult. But that doesn't mean I won't complain about the half-full water balloon shape my breasts have taken on now that we're almost done nursing.

I want to believe that my body is beautiful every single day—even if my tummy is bloated, despite my butt area sagging a little, regardless of the deepening lines around my eyes. And I want desperately for Sweet Pea to think it's normal for a woman to consider herself beautiful.

I know you can't do everything at once. Many years passed between my first jog around the block, which left me red-faced and exhausted, and the "Yes, I can" that led me to my first marathon, subsequent triathlons, and (much) faster marathons. But I don't exactly have years to develop an awesome body image to model for my daughter. I need to start fast, like yesterday.

62

I Hit a Turning Point in My Life When…

A LITTLE MAROON bike changed my life. I bought it with my tax return and a little help from my parents. I enjoyed spin classes, I was injured from running yet planning to do a triathlon someday, and I longed to be able to exercise outside the four stifling walls of my gym. Never mind that I hadn't actually ridden a bike in about a decade. Road biking seemed a fitting hobby. Speaking of fitting, my new sport necessitated I wear the requisite spandex shorts and blindingly bright, loudly patterned jerseys. Also, there were the shoes. Not only did they look ridiculous, but I had to get over the paralyzing fear of my feet being attached to the pedals of a bike with really really skinny tires. But as with any fashion statement—be it bike apparel, jeggings, skinny jeans, what have you—I discovered, if you're going to wear it, you have to own it. Soon enough, I was heading to the grocery store après rides in my spandex like it it was no big whoop. (And in Boulder, Colorado, it isn't. But this was when I lived in Chapel Hill, North Carolina, where it kind of was. A few years later, it was in Rhode Island, where rocking spandex at Stop and Shop qualified me as an alien. Not the illegal kind, the kind from Mars that no one has ever seen.) Once I had the fashion situation under control, there was the small matter of actually riding the bike.

The thing about road biking is that it is almost always done on roads. As in roads where cars drive. This was terrifying to me. So terrifying, in fact, that I would willingly seek out large groups of very fit strangers, whom I would meet in rural areas, and then pedal for dear life for thirty miles or more, just to ride with other people rather than ride alone.

On my first group ride, somewhere between deciding I would rather be anywhere but on my bike and wishing I could just die and let the torture end, one of the guys noticed I was having a hard time.

"Do you need anything?"

I think he was wondering if I'd brought enough water or needed a gel.

Between gasps for air, I said, "An ambulance?"

My ambulance never came, and I had to pedal my sorry self back to my car. This would be the first of many, many times I had to keep going when I really didn't feel like it. Biking taught me perseverance.

A year passed after my ambulance request, and I had gotten rid of not only a few extra pounds but also my fear of clipless pedals (though not without taking down several fellow cyclists and sustaining a bloody gash in my ankle, the result of a poorly managed stop sign situation), as well as my anxiety about riding alone and the dorky visor on my helmet. I'd completed my first metric century (62 miles) and my first sprint triathlon.

I still didn't know how to change a flat tire, however. While biking did not do much to improve my anger problem (my failed attempts to change a tire ended in crying, cursing, screaming, and throwing my tire lever), it did help me hone a much more important skill—getting people to do what I wanted. No, I could not change a tire, but I knew how to bake and could be quite friendly with the menfolk. With a fresh loaf of banana bread in hand, I could flirt my way to the front of the queue at any bike shop and get my flat changed in a hurry.

Inevitably, I had a flat tire during a triathlon and those cute bike mechanics who had always been so generous with their time and their strong, nimble hands were not there to help. A kind pair of sisters who were racing together (P.S. Is that the cutest thing you've ever heard of!?) stopped to help me. I was able to finish but my time was in the toilet. I vowed to learn out how to change a flat myself. So I sat with my bike and a knowledgeable, patient friend until I figured it out. It turned out doing it myself felt a lot better than getting someone else to do it for me, and I didn't even have to turn on the oven (or the charm). From my bike, I learned self-sufficiency.

Now that I had conquered the unthinkable challenge of Changing My Own Flat Tire, the obvious next step was to sign up for an Ironman triathlon, which consists of a 1.2-mile swim, a 112-mile bike, and a 26.2-mile run. Because obviously, if you can change a tire, you can do anything. Actually, I think my main reason for doing my first Ironman was that my friend said she was going to do it, and I'd promised her I would do it if she did. I never said the bike made me smart.

I've ridden that bike up Mount Mitchell, the highest peak of the Appalachian Mountains. I've taken her up Beech Mountain, the legendary training ride that took Lance Armstrong from his battle with cancer to his Tour de France victory. We've ridden through the countryside of southern Spain, including Pico de Veleta, Europe's highest road. We've seen nearly every back road in Rhode Island, as well as parts of Connecticut and

Massachusetts, sometimes all in one day. I've pedaled her across most of the state of Arizona and across the windy plains and over the peaks of Wyoming. We've made it to the top of some of Colorado's most intimidating passes and mountains, including Mount Evans, Wolf Creek Pass, Slumgullion Pass, Rabbit Ears Pass, and the Dallas Divide. We've climbed our way out of Montrose's punishing Black Canyon of the Gunnison. I am not going to tell you how many of these sufferfests were born of peer pressure. Like I said, the bike made me stubborn, not smart.

The bike has made me a lot of things—strong, fit, disciplined, tenacious, and fearless among them, but most of all, it made and continues to make me happy. Riding my bike with the wind in my face and the sun on my back never fails to make me smile. The bone-aching fatigue of a long day in the saddle makes my heart sing. The out-of-this-world deliciousness of a medium rare cheeseburger after one of those days is enough to make this agnostic pretty sure god exists.

Resting my hands on a steering wheel and keeping one foot on the gas will never be more fun than hanging onto the handlebars and pushing both feet down on the pedals. It doesn't matter if I'm heading up Lefthand Canyon or taking the bike path to the library with Sweet Pea in the Burley. When I'm riding my bike, I feel like humming a song. Not that you could necessarily recognize it. I never said the bike made me a better singer—just a little better, braver of a person.

63

In My Next Life...

IN MY NEXT life, I would like to return to earth as my husband. Is that even possible, to come back in a reincarnated state as someone who is alive right now? I just want to know what it feels like to be him. You might think I would have a pretty good idea, considering we have been super serious since we met more than five years ago, have been married for three years, and have a child together. He's one of my favorite people ever. But sometimes he baffles me and that is why I want to get inside his head.

He never, ever irons his shirts (except for weddings, and I can't confirm that he did this before we met). He gets mad at me for ironing them or for even throwing them in the dryer for five minutes to minimize wrinkles (although he doesn't know I actually do this with his button-down shirts 99 percent of the time. *Hey, babe... Surprise!*). He says he can't be bothered spending any extra time on his appearance because it's just not important. I say I feel like my head is going to explode when he shoves the clothing I've lovingly, smoothly folded into a ball and throws it willy-nilly into the closet. I've never actually exploded. I've yelled a lot and resigned myself to folding and putting away all the laundry.

But can you imagine all the time I would have if I weren't spending any of my precious minutes folding or ironing clothes, nagging my husband about clothes, or changing my own outfit multiple times before leaving the house? I could probably run twenty more miles a week, blog one or two more times a week, and finish some of the projects I started nearly a year ago, like refinishing an end table and sewing some really cute bibs.

Also, he dresses Sweet Pea in whatever has the fewest fasteners and is clean, with little regard for what goes together as an outfit, whereas I dress her in whatever is most cute, with utmost respect for the Sanctity of Her Outfits. She has a lot of outfits that came together as a matched set, and if you put the top of one matched set with some random bottom, then one day you're going to come across the bottom of the matched set but you won't have a top that goes with it, which means you can't put her in that bottom until the laundry has been done, and she grows way too fast to waste chances to wear cute, matching outfits.

What would it feel like to go out with Sweet Pea, both of us in functional, if wrinkled, not necessarily matching garb and not even *care*. It would probably give me energy to care about things that actually matter... *OK, Dan? Are you reading this? I admit it. These things don't actually matter.*

Also, Dan isn't all about a meal having mostly protein, some carbs, and a little fat, like I am. Unless it's before a workout—then my meal has to be practically all simple carbs. Dan just eats food. We'll be on a bike ride and fifteen miles in he's like, "Let's stop for a burrito. I'm starving!" and I'm like, "What did you have for breakfast?" and he says, "A peach and some green beans." Because that's just what he felt like eating. And I'm not just saying he would maybe eat something that ridiculous. He actually ate that before a long ride one time.

Me? I have to have my instant oatmeal with a splash of milk, a handful of raisins, and a sprinkling of slivered almonds. Also, I need coffee of the exact right strength with half-and-half. Not milk, not Coffee-mate, just half-and-half, preferably organic. If I don't have this meal before a bike ride, then…then I don't even know what would happen because I always have this meal before a bike ride. I can't imagine what it would feel like to be fancy-free, opening the refrigerator and just eating whatever looks good. And I don't really want to take any chances and try it sometime. See, that's why I need to come back as Dan in another life. It won't work otherwise, because probably I would just start riding my bike after an alternative breakfast and be like, "My tummy feels weird" and "I have no energy because I ate a stupid breakfast!"

Another thing about Dan that I can't quite wrap my head around: The man never wears a watch. I, on the other hand, wear a watch all the time, even to sleep. If I wake up in the middle of the night, I need to know what time it is. I am very, very nearsighted, so I have to hold my wrist up about one inch away from my face so I can see the time, otherwise I will probably explode from not knowing what time it is. During the day, I can usually guess what time it is within ten minutes, but I wear a watch anyway. This discrepancy in watch-wearing habits has, believe it or not, been a source of tension in our marriage.

Did you know the simple words "You have no idea what time it is" can be hurled at a spouse like a grenade? I have found that if spoken loudly enough with a certain minimum threshold of sleep deprivation, these words are potentially quite dangerous. Like when you're exhausted and your baby is not doing what the books said she would do—those books that made you a parenting expert back when you knew everything, before you became a parent, at which point you realized you knew nothing—and obviously your baby is not sleeping like she is supposed to because you're not doing what the books said to do, so you are trying to do what they say, but when you've been out and you come home and you're like, "How long has the baby been up?" and your husband says, "I don't know," and then you say, "Well, what time did she wake up from her nap?" and he's like, "I didn't look at the time," and then you feel like you want to explode, but you don't, so instead you yell, "GET A WATCH! OH MY GOD!" but even though he never did start wearing a watch, it's all good because that was so 2012 and you're in a completely different place now, which means you can laugh at how uptight you were about the whole sleep thing.

Seriously, it would probably be freeing to not wear a watch. I might like it. I think I will try this one day. When I am reincarnated as my husband, that is.

64

Mission Impossible: Waking Up

YOU MIGHT THINK it's easy to be a night person, but you'd be wrong. It would seem reasonable that if the most dreadful part of your day is the simple act of waking up, HURRAY, you've conquered your most challenging battle before the crack of 7:55 PBT/5:55 BST (Pre-Baby Time/Baby Standard Time) and it's all downhill from there.

What's so hard about peeling one's eyelids open, getting out from under the snuggly warmth of 500-threadcount cotton sheets, and standing up to greet the day? For starters, everything. Let me break it down for you.

SCENARIO #1: WAKE UP WITH ALARM CLOCK (A.K.A PUBLIC ENEMY #1)
SET ALARM CLOCK the night before with master plan in mind. Allow time for 8-mile tempo run, stretching, core work, leisurely drink of water, and shower before baby handoff when husband leaves for work. When alarm goes off, press snooze before first conscious thought forms. If had to choose between oxygen and snooze button at this point, would definitely choose snooze.

Decide stretching can wait till another day. Nine minutes later, alarm sounds. Reach for snooze button before becoming aware that the sound is supposed to inspire wakefulness. Need to make it stop. Return to drowsing. Decide core work not necessary today. Nine minutes later, alarm sounds. Arm extends toward snooze button reflexively. Feel OK about shortening 8-mile tempo run to 6.5-mile run.

Nine minutes later, alarm sounds. Resign self to getting up eventually and running with baby in BOB stroller. Will do tempo run tomorrow, slow jog with baby in BOB stroller today.

Nine minutes later, alarm sounds again. Rub eyes, stand up and feel guilty and ashamed of self for not following through with plans because only losers do not follow through with plans. Lack of discipline is obvious sign of being a shitty person.

Have first sip of coffee. Decide maybe can live with self after all.

Scenario 2: Wake Up with Baby Crying

HEAR "EH-EH" FROM baby's room. Hope whining will die down and baby will fall back asleep. "Eh-eh" escalates to whine, which escalates to cry. Hope cry will stop after five minutes. Cry escalates to madness within three minutes, then abates. Fall back to sleep. Cry starts again. Cry becomes singing. Fall back asleep. Cry starts again.

After thirty minutes, decide continued taunting cannot be tolerated and retrieve baby and bring her to big bed in hopes of quiet mom-baby snuggle time. Feel baby's full weight resting on your throat. Reposition baby without opening eyes. Baby scratches your face with the toenail she has refused to let anyone trim. Place baby lovingly on chest, where offending toenail is far from your face. Baby gropes your nipples like drunk frat guy. Can't take it anymore. Get up.

Feel nostalgic for the times when baby would entertain self in crib for first hour of day. Wonder which of your parental failings have resulted in baby's inability to play alone.

Take first sip of coffee. Decide maybe you don't totally suck at parenting.

SCENARIO 3: WAKE UP NATURALLY (OBV A FANTASY)
MERELY CONSIDERING THIS causes urge to weep for pre-baby life, in which weekend mornings were often spent lazing in bed with husband and Styles section of Sunday *New York Times*, sometimes coffee. Feel guilty for yearning for old life, especially upon noting your beautiful, healthy daughter is one of life's most precious gifts and you are total ungrateful asshole. Repeat cycle of self-loathing/coffee drinking.

65

If You Ever Plan to Live with Me, You Need to Know This

I HAVE A bad habit of acting like a lunatic. Even when my household objects cooperate, I am about as calm as a caffeinated toddler. But when they don't, my rage knows no bounds.

Yes, I am the crazed lady you backed away from before we made eye contact at the Redbox kiosk last summer. Maybe you saw me fumbling around, trying to jam my DVD into the slot. Except it wouldn't go. I shoved straight. I shoved at an angle. I shoved at a different angle. I tried concentrating. I tried relaxing.

I tried snarling, "Goddamnit, get in there!" It still wouldn't go.
I tried sliding the other side in first.
"Jesus H. Christ, GO!"
I went back to the original side and gave it a hard shove. Still nothing. I was hot. I was hungry. I was about to incur another day's worth of charges. I slammed the front surface of the DVD against the machine. "Motherfucker, get in the box!"

I took a stealth look around, hoping no one I knew witnessed my crazy. I kicked the machine. I wished I hadn't worn flip-flops. "Shit!"

I took a deep breath. I took a long blink. I asked a passing stranger what I was doing wrong. She kindly explained that I hadn't pressed the touchscreen where it says "Press here to start."

I wish I could say that was the time I went batshit crazy on a thing and laugh about how crazy I was that day, but that was just one of many times. I am an equal opportunity inanimate object hater. Perhaps Dan recalls the time I called him in tears about my closet doors. (At the time, we were engaged, so he can't say he didn't know what he signed up for when we got married.) The closet doors had a chronic condition that caused them to come off the track. The root cause of their condition was, no doubt, my dirt-cheap rent. Totally tragic, I know. I called Dan after I had screamed every cuss word I knew and before I had this conversation with my landlady:

Me: **The closet doors keep falling off the track.**
Landlady: **I will have the maintenance guy come out again.**
Me [in a severely bitchy tone]: **Um, who *is* the maintenance guy?**
Landlady: **My husband.**
Me [sheepishly]: **Oh, cool.**

Other standout performances of unleashing my fury on defenseless things include Pam's Low Back versus the Ten-Year-Old Pack and Play, The Tale of the Unruly MacBook, The iPad That Would Not Behave, The Mystery of the Nearly Impossible to Manipulate Bike Tire Which Was Later Found to Be Inside Out, and the latest, The Night the Internet Wouldn't Let Pam

Copy and Paste Her New Temporary Banking Password Into the Password Field.

I'm not proud that I've verbally abused, kicked, hit, and jabbed household objects. I'm trying to control myself. Believe it or not, I am really good about taking a deep breath before I completely lose my shit.

66

Reflections

I SPEND MORE time than I'd like to admit looking in the mirror. Brown boots versus black? One-piece or two-piece? When did that vertical wrinkle show up right next to my mouth and why is it only on the right side of my face? My husband will call out, "When are you coming to bed? Are you looking in the mirror?"

"No. Yes. I'm...making decisions!" I'll yell back.

For someone who has made a pastime of prancing around in the mirror, I have only just begun to see myself.

"Pamela?" The slight nurse practically whispers my name as she approaches me in the waiting room. She introduces herself, eyes downcast, her petite frame lost in her baggy army green scrubs. She asks me to step on the scale, her voice barely rising above a whisper. She pulls a thermometer out of her pocket and mumbles something as she steps toward me. Before she sticks the instrument in my ear, I stop her.

"I can barely hear you." My tone is not gentle. Yet I know exactly what she plans to do with her thermometer. Why am I being such a bitch? Her only crime is shyness. I ask myself whether

I would behave this way in the presence of my eighteen-month-old daughter and immediately soften.

Before I became a mother, I'd go to the grocery story and help myself to the random peanut butter–covered pretzels, chocolate-covered espresso beans, and yogurt-covered raisins in the bulk aisle that careless customers spilled into the plastic grid underneath the dispensers. If they didn't get into my mouth first, they were headed for the trash. I wasn't doing anything wrong, I told myself.

Then I had Sweet Pea. I can lie to myself, but I cannot lie to my child. These days, I look longingly at the appetizing food in the bulk aisle. Once in a while I purchase a half a pound of that sweet goodness, but I no longer sneak the forgotten pieces into my mouth.

When I feel myself getting impatient with the cashier at the drugstore, the front desk girl at the gym, the customer service representative on the phone, or one of the roof guys that leaves us a card just about every week, in case we weren't aware that our 1960s T-lock tile roof is way overdue to be replaced, I take a deep breath and fight the urge to speak sharply. Though I am grossly underqualified for the position, one of my essential job functions as a mother is to teach my daughter how to interact with the world.

With her little eyes trained on me, I no longer lean on the excuses I used to make. *He is stupid. She is slow. I don't have time for this.* Who am I to feel like I am better than these people who are only doing their jobs? What right do I have to give them attitude?

Looking at myself through my daughter's eyes, I am ashamed of my sense of entitlement. I know there are certain things I may not be able to avoid passing on to her—a lifetime of taking her pants to be shortened, an endless search for the perfect hair product, and an eyeglass prescription so strong that even the optometrist raises her eyebrows at it.

But I will do everything in my power to keep Sweet Pea from absorbing the feeling that the world owes her something. While I was busy choosing between the cardigan versus the jean jacket, I never saw how bad this ugly attitude looked on me. Until I became her mother.

To my daughter, I am the cool girl who does everything right. She tries on my shoes. She puts my hair elastics around her wrist. She sets my sunglasses on top of her head. She parrots my expressions and inflections. Apparently, I walk around the house saying "OK" to no one in particular. When she sits in the cart at Marshall's, she reaches her chubby arm out to touch everything in her reach, just to feel the fabric as she goes by. Just like I do.

Motherhood smashed the backlit skinny mirror I used to rely on and left in its place a magnifying mirror and a 1,000-watt fluorescent bulb. I don't miss my old mirror. It made me feel good about myself, but what I was seeing was an illusion. I need the mirror motherhood gave me to see who I really am and start becoming the person my daughter needs me to be.

67

Just a Basement

FOR THE LAST few days, Sweet Pea has been obsessed with my old charm necklace and a My Little Pony, or "hush." (In case you're not bilingual, that's toddler-speak for *horse*.) I found these relics of the eighties when I was schlepping load upon load of stuff up from our basement to higher ground as it became inevitable that the flooring would have to be replaced. I plucked these treasures out, hoping they might occupy my daughter the way they occupied me when I was little and my parents were in a frenzy about flooding in the basement. As a kid, I never understood what the big deal was. If anything, I imagined a flood would be a cause for celebration, because when else could you go swimming in the street? And I secretly thought my parents might have been a little overdramatic. There was never so much as a wading-pool water level in our basement, never mind a so-called flood.

I walked downstairs to grab some laundry in the basement Wednesday night, thinking this was going to be the last thing I did before crawling into bed. My pj's were on, my contacts were out, and I'd hardly been able to keep my head up since dinner time.

When I got to the bottom of the stairs, my feet were instantly cold and wet. I knew I would not be going to bed anytime soon.

I texted Dan "Please come home ASAP. Big flood basement." In a heartbeat, I switched from sleep mode to turbo mode. I grabbed every spare towel in the house and threw them at the mess. I called our neighbors to see if they had a shop vac we could borrow. They didn't, but they have a kid who was available to sit at our house while Sweet Pea slept, so I could run to Home Depot before they closed.

I hopped in my car and raced to Home Depot. And by raced I mean drove like a total grandma, because I do anyway, and the roads were shiny with fresh rain. Many times, a wall of water at least four feet tall rose up on either side of my car as I passed through puddles that might be more aptly described as small ponds. I grabbed the last shop vac Home Depot had and headed home.

I know my astute readers may be wondering why Dan didn't pick up the shop vac on his way home. He had ridden his bike. He thought he'd be OK because he had rain pants. No one predicted we would have rain like this.

We vacuumed for hours, but we hardly made a dent and called it quits by 11:30. The next day, after lots of vacuuming and lots more rain, we waved our white flag. Water had poured in through our window wells, which we were now scooping out by the five-gallon bucketful every couple of hours. Water continued to seep in through the foundation as the rain hammered on.

On Friday we finally heard back from the only one of several water damage remediation places we'd called. They were willing to remove all the carpet and dry out the drywall for $3,000, but Dan thought perhaps he could do it himself. Again, my astute readers might wonder, "But won't insurance pay for it?" No, no it won't. We don't have flood insurance. We're not in a flood plain and our climate is known for being optimal for curly hair—dry.

So, between Friday, Saturday, and today, with help from friends and family, we did it! We removed all of the carpet, all of the foam pad, all the baseboards, and lots and lots of wet drywall. And by we I pretty much mean Dan. I played the supporting roles of First Responder, Water Scooper, Stuff Carrier, Meal Cooker, Child Watcher, and Pizza Orderer, but Dan was the star as the Lead Water Damage Avenger.

At this point, we are glad we beat the clock, as we got the wet stuff out quickly, which should mean we will not have a mold problem. Our stuff is intact, not that any of it was really that important. I am actually looking forward to going through and paring it down, as it's all in a big heap and will eventually have to go back to some semblance of order, once we sort out our drainage issues and put down some new floor. And I'm pretty excited about putting down some new hardwood vinyl flooring. Sounds weird, looks awesome.

We are glad it's not worse. One of my coworkers lost her house and nearly died trying to get out. So many people in surrounding areas were evacuated or don't have power. People living in the mountains normally forty minutes from town have lost access to the main road, which is not passable. So our basement is messed up—big deal.

We got a chance to go for a walk during a respite from the rain Friday evening. All the neighbors were out, comparing notes. We met people we'd never seen before. When they asked where we lived, we said, "We're the house with no front yard, just garden." And everyone was like, "Oh, that's you." Yep, we're the hippies with the amazing tomatoes, cucumbers, zucchini, squash, basil, and cantaloupe.

My mom asked me if it was anything like the flooding we used to have in our basement when I was a kid. I laughed and shook my head. I held the phone between my shoulder and my ear as Sweet Pea held my leg with one arm and her hush and charm necklace with the other.

"Mom, I have no idea! When I was a kid, it wasn't my problem."

68

Letting Go

DO YOU EVER have an argument with your husband and a day or two later you can't even remember what it was about? You remember how mad you were, how upset he was, but if, say, it came down to some government interrogation, the second they hinted at torture you'd agree it was about the first thing they suggested, just because you didn't have any better ideas and also, water boarding? No thanks.

This happens to me all the time. Not being interrogated; I mean having no idea what the fight was even about. I'm sure that's something I should probably meditate about or something, but for now I'm just going to add that to my to-do list.

Like, the other night. I have no idea what happened. I'm sure I started it, because that's how I roll, but how we got from the beginning to me wrapping my baby heads in layers of newspaper, I can't exactly say. I think I might have accused Dan of hoarding too much old, useless stuff. It might also have been the same day I dug out a My Little Pony and my old charm necklace from my childhood for our daughter to play with.

All I remember for sure is Dan suddenly turning bright red and screaming something about how he can't stand my stuff either, especially the ugly babies that he didn't want to look at ever again. Then he turned and, without even using a step stool or a chair or anything—yeah, I might be a little jealous—reached up with his long arms to the archway at the entrance to our kitchen and took my chalkware down. I half expected him to throw them, letting them crash into an infinity of flesh-colored pieces as they hit the tile floor, pieces that we would end up having to sweep up, laughing as we emptied the dustpan into the trash. But throwing stuff isn't his style. In fact, raising his voice is not his style. Normally, he is the calm to my crazy.

But this time Dan had had enough. It had been a long weekend, most of which he'd spent removing carpet and drywall from our flooded basement. And I had not the sense to avoid antagonizing the good man who had been doing manual labor all weekend.

He was already at his edge when I started in about his stuff, so it should not have surprised me when he lost it. He was tired of my rant, and he was sick of looking at the strange babies that had decorated nearly all of my apartments since college. For more than three years they had decorated our kitchen. For more than three years, he quietly tolerated them while I loved them.

I thought they were quirky. He thought they were disturbing.

There they sat, on the kitchen table. The ceramic, bald, crying baby and the baby with a top hat and a pipe sticking out of its mouth.

Neither of us said a word.

I broke the silence with a laugh. "Wow, you really hate the babies. I didn't know you hated them so much. I guess I can let them go."

69

Why Real Parents Don't Round: Air Travel with a Toddler

"Don't touch my eyes."
"Quick, do a Google Image search for pigs!"
"That's my neck. Gentle on my neck."
"Why are you showing me Wheat Thins? She asked for GOLD. FISH."
"WHY WON'T WUBZY LOAD!?"
"I SAID don't touch my neck."

These are some of the comments I made on a flight back from California this weekend. Actually, calling them comments makes them sound much more sophisticated than they actually are. Let's start over. I actually said this stuff. There, that feels more authentic.

Every time I fly with Sweet Pea, it is the worst flight ever. Until the next time, of course. Because, the next time, she is a little bit older, a little bit bigger, and a little bit louder. Which equals a lot worse.

The infant who used to happily sleep, cuddle, and nurse in flight morphed, practically overnight, into a caged animal when confined to my lap at thirty thousand feet. Last summer, when Sweet Pea was a sweet, bald five-month-old, strangers asked to hold her because she was so cute. I got to go to the bathroom by myself and even read part of a magazine uninterrupted. This summer, strangers asked to hold my out-of-control toddler because after nearly four hours, they pitied me. With the brief respite, I had time to retrieve a new board book from my diaper bag before she was so graciously handed back to me.

This weekend, the flight was a mere two hours and fifteen minutes, and I had Dan with me. It would be relatively easy, right? Wrong. There is a reason I mention the flight was two hours *and fifteen minutes*. Ask any runner how long a marathon is. It's 26.2 miles. Not 26. Those last 0.2 miles are as painful as the first 26 miles combined. And those last fifteen minutes of a two-hour-and-fifteen-minute flight? As aggravating as the first two hours combined. If you meet a runner or a parent who rounds, you would be wise to question this person's legitimacy.

Take Scenario A: Your toddler wants Goldfish twenty-four minutes into the flight. It is kind of annoying that the child is in your lap and you have to move her to your husband's lap in order to reach into your diaper bag, which is stowed, per flight attendants' orders, neatly beneath the seat in front of you, to reach said Goldfish. Meanwhile, your toddler doesn't want to go to your husband, so she's crying and clinging to your shoulder, even as you remain less than an inch away from her. You are thankful that your husband is along to share the moment.

Now let's review Scenario B: Your toddler wants Goldfish two hours and six minutes into the flight. She's in the Ergo Carrier because you are about to lose your mind over the constant struggle between your will (to keep her in your lap while the seatbelt sign is on) and her will (to run up and down the aisle while intermittently demanding "UP!"). Your child is facing you in the Ergo, and she is taking a break from the game where she jerks her body quickly from extreme left to extreme right in an attempt to play peekaboo through the cracks between the seats with the stranger sitting behind you. (BTW, who named this thing the Ergo Carrier?) She is demanding Goldfish.

"Doh fish. DOH. FISH."

Normally you would insist, "Goldfish, what?" until she responded with "Doh fish peez." Normally you are not trapped with her in a confined space. You are basically her hostage at this point, willing to give into any and all of her demands, as quickly as possible, to maintain peace. You have no power. You have only snacks and an iPad that is supposedly connected to Wi-Fi but won't actually load any TV shows.

You hand her two Goldfish at a time, which she chews, loudly and slowly, with her mouth open, one inch from your face. Small pieces of bright orange mush form a mustache on her upper lip and a soul patch on her chin, which is perilously close to your chest. You've never felt airsick before, but now you are starting to wish you hadn't ruined that vomit bag with your bright idea to use it as a puppet an hour ago. Everyone warns new parents about close encounters with poop, vomit, and urine. No one ever says anything about close-range Goldfish eating. You are thankful you didn't bring Munchos. (Goldfish at least pretend to be made of cheese. What actual food are Munchos masquerading as?)

Eventually (after two hours and, *ahem*, fifteen minutes) we arrive at our destination. We arrive safely and without incident, unless you count the fact that the iPad would not show us any TV shows. I know I should be grateful. And I am. I really am. I'm just saying, next time I will take precautions to make sure The iPad TV Show Plan is totally fail-safe.

70

Traveling with My Toddler: Heaven Is Having My Lap to Myself

THIS PAST HOLIDAY season an amazing thing happened. I enjoyed air travel with my toddler. I even read a few chapters of my book on the plane.

See, I used to love planes. I loved everything about air travel. I liked to buy a magazine, a processed snack, and a four-dollar bottle of water at the airport. I loved people watching. I loved the anticipation of knowing you would be in another state, physically and mentally, in mere hours. I especially loved the chance to read without interruption on the plane. I have a distinct memory of hitting the tarmac at Boston Logan after a four-hour flight and wishing we weren't there yet because I *needed* to finish my novel and I had only thirty pages to go. (It was *Big Girl Small*, in case you were wondering.)

And then I had a child.

Instead of relishing a copy of *Real Simple*, I bust open a copy of *Sky Mall* and scour it for pictures of dogs with my toddler on my lap. I bring a lot of snack food, and I ask for two of whatever they are offering on the plane because Ritz Bits and Lorna Doone cookies turn out to be very effective pacifiers for my twenty-one-month-old. I don't have time to buy expensive water because I'm busy waiting for the handicapped stall to open up so I can fit in there with a stroller and then do a quick diaper change before we board. I hesitate to fill my Nalgene bottle at the water fountain because I would rather not have to choose between going to the restroom on the plane while my toddler is unattended or inviting her to keep me company in the lav. I no longer people watch. Instead I must channel all my powers of observation on my toddler, who needs to walk as much as possible at the gate before she is confined to my lap for hours. It's hard to people watch when you're busy person watching and said person stands two feet tall and possesses the disposition of a friendly drunk.

So neither Dan nor I were thrilled at the prospect of flying from Denver to Boston for either Thanksgiving or Christmas this year. I love my family dearly, but this year I chose my mental health over my family and decided to stay local for the holidays.

I did, however, take Sweet Pea back East to visit my folks for a week right after Thanksgiving. Our tickets were cheap. The airports were relatively easy to manage given that it wasn't a holiday. Dan decided to stay back so he could save up his vacation time for when the baby comes. I was nervous about such a long flight alone with my toddler. Since she's still under two, she would be on my lap. Denver to Boston is quite a long way, even in a jet plane. It's even longer when there's a thirty-pound human on your lap.

Despite having stocked up on Goldfish and downloading several episodes of *Sesame Street* and some cat cartoon on the iPad, I worried that perhaps the two hundred dollars it would have cost to buy my child her own seat would have been more than worth it. How could I have put a price on having my lap to myself? I had never really considered the monetary worth of my personal space before.

But the heavens shone upon me on this trip, as I was blessed with the good fortune of an empty middle seat in our row. Both ways. We flew Southwest, the only airline I know of where people can choose not to sit next to you because you look annoying, you're too big, you're eating a tuna fish sandwich, or, in my case, because you have a toddler on your lap. I know Southwest reminds a lot of people of a crappy, flying Greyhound bus, but while the haters hate, I will fly with my twenty-one-month-old in her own seat that I didn't have to pay for, thank you very much.

Heaven is not having to share a seat with your toddler for four hours. I am agnostic, but I may reconsider things this holiday season.

71

Why I Chose Home Birth

A FRIEND INVITED me to the home birth of her child a few years ago. It was a really special—dare I say, spiritual—experience to witness a life coming into this world. Not to get too woo-woo on you, but it was life affirming. You know how you feel at a wedding when they say "You may kiss the bride"? It was kind of like that, times a thousand.

Although I felt home birth worked out well for my friend, it was definitely not something I would consider for myself. When it was my turn to have a baby, I would do it in a hospital, where all the necessary technology and trained medical personnel would be available were anything to go wrong. I just didn't think there was any reason I would want to risk my or my baby's health by giving birth at home.

When Dan and I decided that we wanted to have a baby, I did what comes naturally to me—I read and I planned. Everything I read led me to conclude that perhaps I would not feel as comfortable in a hospital as I had thought. I learned that there were many interventions and restrictions that were not research based and were not necessarily useful and that sometimes they were uncomfortable for the mother. For example, many hospitals have a policy of no eating or drinking for laboring women. It is my understanding that this is in case you would have to have general anesthesia for an emergency C-section. In this case, anything in your stomach becomes an aspiration risk. That is well and good, except they seldom put you under for a C-section these days. Also, many hospitals use electronic fetal monitoring. This requires you to move carefully or not much at all so that it stays in place. It has not, however, been proven to increase the chances of a healthy outcome. There were many other things I read that did not sit well with me, but those are just a couple that come to mind.

The reading I did led me to believe that giving birth in the hospital opens the door for medical intervention, and once you begin with one intervention, it often leads to a cascade of other interventions, which heightens your chances of requiring a C-section. I knew I wanted to avoid a C-section, and I did not want to do anything that would facilitate one becoming a necessity. I also knew that I did not want an epidural or pain medication. I wanted to know what birth really felt like. What I had read assured me that under the right circumstances (privacy, no feeling of being rushed, being in a position that allows gravity to help, in the presence of people whom you know and trust, not having many people present), a woman whose pregnancy is considered low risk is usually well equipped to deliver naturally. I considered giving birth a rite of passage, and I wanted to experience it.

Also, I scream bloody murder when I stub my toe. I take three Advil at the first sign of a headache. I really enjoyed the Versed they used when I had my wisdom teeth removed. I didn't think I would avoid an epidural if one was available.

I have worked in hospitals for ten years, and I know things about hospitals I wish I didn't know. I know not everyone washes their hands as thoroughly or as often as they should. I know how easy it is to mistake one patient for another when you're busy and rushed. I know how easily you can forget the details of someone's medical history or be unaware of them in the first place because of incomplete or nonexistent medical records. I know how clueless and arrogant medical residents can be.

And I know how angry I get as a patient when some person pokes at me without even introducing him- or herself or stating what they are doing there. Seriously, someone whose name I did not know once stuck a probe in my eyeball without even warning me, and it really pissed me off. (Turned out it wasn't to be mean, it was to check my corneal pressure. Who knew?)

I couldn't imagine delivering a baby in the company of strangers, especially strangers who might treat me more like a patient than a person. And what if my doctor wasn't on call when I delivered? What if I liked my nurse, but she had to leave when her shift was complete and I didn't like my new nurse? I wanted to give birth in the presence of a professional I trusted, someone I had a relationship with.

With all this in mind, it seemed my only option was, in fact, the home birth I never thought I would have. That is how I went from definitely not ever having a home birth to having a home birth.

I am pretty sure I wouldn't have had the same experience had I given birth the traditional way, with a doctor or a midwife in the hospital. For one thing, everyone predicted the baby would be large. The acupuncturist, a former midwife, estimated eight pounds or so. My midwife predicted seven and a half to eight pounds. At an ultrasound performed the day I went into labor, the OB acknowledged that midwives are generally more accurate than ultrasound in predicting size, but his image indicated an eight-and-a-half-pound baby. I was the only one who was convinced I was having a six-pounder. I just thought there was no way a baby that large was in me. I was 5'0" and 115 pounds before I got pregnant. So there was the big baby part.

More important, there was the fact that I was long overdue by the time I went into labor—twelve days, to be exact. By the time the baby was born, it was a full two weeks beyond my due date. I wonder how many traditional doctors or midwives would have let my pregnancy go that long. Meanwhile, I was healthy, there was every reason to believe the baby was healthy, and as it turned out, she came on her own when she was ready, even if it was more than fashionably late.

I think that if I had been induced, the labor and delivery would have turned out very differently. As it was, I had a long labor (thirty hours total). I tore slightly, I healed normally, and we had no problems with breastfeeding or postpartum depression. I could not have asked for a more positive birth experience.

For so many reasons, I am thankful that I went the home birth route. At the birth were my midwife, her assistant, Dan, and my mom. I never had to get in the car while I was having contractions. I was never told that I was exhausted. I was never poked or prodded by someone I'd never seen before. I never felt scared.

It lasted forever, and it was one moment. It was the worst thing and the best thing I have ever been through. It was a process that I had to surrender to and a process I was not sure I could endure. I will always consider it a peak experience of my life.

Yeah, there was blood in the birth tub. Don't worry, everyone was fine. Birth is just bloody.

72

A Primer for Making Small Talk with Pregnant Ladies

I AM NOW every-stranger-feels-the-need-to-ask-me-if-I-am-almost-ready-which-I-am-not-thank-you-very-much weeks pregnant, a.k.a. thirty weeks. That means nearly three months to go. Three months until my body is mine again, except not, because nursing and holding an infant, plus managing the constant and ever-changing demands of my mean boss toddler.

In case you feel compelled to make small talk with a pregnant woman, here are some things to keep in mind.

What you say: **Wow! You look like you're about ready to go!**
What she hears: **OMG, you're huge!**

What you say [in line for ladies room]: **Would you like to go ahead of me?**
What she hears: **Angels singing**

A Primer for Making Small Talk with Pregnant Ladies

What you say: **When is your due date?**
What she hears: **You need to squeeze that baby out asap because you look uncomfortably HUGE.**

What you say: **You look great!**
What she hears: **Angels singing**

What you say: **Whoa, are you sure it's not twins?**
What she hears: **Jesus H. Christ, you are huge.**

What you say: **That is a great belly!**
What she hears: **Angels singing**

What you say: **Is this your first?**
What she hears: **Do you have any freaking clue what you are doing?**

What you say: **Are you sure you're allowed to eat/drink/do that?**
What she hears: **The slurping sound of a sponge sucking up every last drop of fun**

What you say: **Seriously, you don't even look pregnant from the back.**
What she hears: **Angels singing**

Obviously, I jest. Mostly. Remember, pregnant women are people too, except they are carrying the extra weight of a baby elephant, they are exhausted but can't sleep because of heartburn, and they are crazy hormonal. Tread lightly, wouldja?

73

No, I'm Not Pregnant with Triplets, but Thanks for Asking

MAYBE I WAS asking for it because I was wearing a two-piece swimsuit. Or perhaps it was that the body revealed by my skimpy attire begged for attention—with its abundance of stretch marks, silvery-taupe in hue, gently drifting across my pregnant belly in horizontal wavy lines. And let's not forget the belly itself—perfectly round, except where the baby's butt creates its own little bump in the upper left quadrant (that's my left, your right), taut as the balloons the nice man at the liquor store blows up for Sweet Pea, and just about the same size.

I debated heavily whether or not to even go to the pool in the first place. On one hand, I was tired in a special thirty-nine-weeks-pregnant-and-carrying-an-extra-thirty-five-pounds kind of way. On the other hand, I hadn't done anything resembling exercise in several days, and I had scored a soon-to-expire guest pass to a fancy gym with a beautiful outdoor pool.. It was a gorgeous day, and Sweet Pea and Dan were content to stay home and dig in the garden without me.

So I swam in the heated, salinated outdoor pool in the sunshine for about twenty-five minutes. I even managed a few flip turns. When I could no longer stand the fact that I had to pee and I got a cramp, I climbed out, toweled off, used the restroom, and relaxed on a chaise lounge.

I got out my phone and did a Google search for "positive birth stories." I thought it might be worthwhile to attempt to get in the mood to give birth, but I'm afraid it's just like working out, scrubbing the toilet, writing, or having sex—you can't wait for the mood to strike. You just have to do it and you'll be glad you did afterward.

There I sat, searching for inspiration, when suddenly standing before me was this lady I'd never seen before in a blue and black Speedo. She was probably in her forties. I wish I could remember any other detail of her appearance but I cannot. It didn't occur to me at the time that it would be nice to note some identifying features for when I would write about this.

Looking down at me, she said, with shock and wonder,

"Are you having *triplets*?!"

My dad is fond of reminding me there is nothing new under the sun, but apparently there is. Though I have written about the crazy shit people will say to pregnant women, I had not heard this before.

I met her eyes and paused for a moment, drawing on muscle memory from my teenage years to give her the dirtiest look I could muster and the most hostile tone I could convey in a mere syllable.

"No."

I then looked down at my phone in my continued search for inspiration, assuming this was the universal sign for "Please do not speak to me anymore." But she persisted.

"Well, you look great!"

I supposed she realized her gaffe and was trying to make amends. Certainly, I've engaged my mouth before my brain could catch up many a time. I could relate. Sort of. So I smiled and thanked her and promptly looked back down at my phone. I was busy searching for inspiration, damnit. She wasn't done yet, though.

"You must be due, like, *any minute*, then!"

I smiled again, this time with my mouth pinched. Why does everyone think this is such a novel, interesting thing to say? I have been hearing this since March. Enough already.

"Yep, any minute."

I looked down at my phone again. This conversation now resembled the life of my dog in the weeks before she was euthanized—painful, devoid of any joy or meaning. Yet she could not let it go.

"You look so ready and together!"

I was wearing my teal two-piece Speedo from two seasons ago, my hair was in a half-wet/half-dry state of limbo, I had no makeup on, and there were goggle marks around my eyes. I do not remember the last time a razor made contact with my legs (bending is just not worth it), and as for my bikini line—I have not been able to see it in months, so I can't really speak to its condition.

All of that said, I am not trying to tell you I look like a big, gross whale. Not to brag, but my face looks exactly the same as before I was pregnant (thin and free of acne), and I haven't sprouted any odd moles, rashes, or patches of hair where patches of hair aren't supposed to be, which are things people like to warn pregnant women about. And while I did recently treat myself to a manicure and a pedicure, I wasn't sure where this woman got the idea, just from interrogating me for a few minutes, that I was "ready and together."

She pressed on, "You really seem ready. Do you feel ready?"

I was ready for her to walk away from me.

"I guess so, yeah." I put my head down again, and when I looked up, she was gone.

I did end up finding a decent birth story to read, though I'm still not entirely inspired. Inspiration or not, this is happening. And when it's over, I will be able to go out in public and freely make eye contact with strangers, even at the pool. How I look forward to that day.

74

The Bizarro World Golden Rule

YESTERDAY MORNING I set my alarm for 6 a.m. All I wanted was an hour or so to myself before people would start needing me. (Although, who are we kidding; I'm on call 24/7. Or my breasts are, anyway, with a newborn in the mix.)

The baby was up at 4:45 to nurse. When I put her back down at five, I felt strangely energetic. It was the first time in a long time the baby had slept this many hours (SIX POINT SEVEN FIVE HOURS! HALLELUJAH!) in a row. I had every reason to stay up and drink a hot, uninterrupted cup of coffee or blog or go for a run or take a shower or perhaps do all of these before the clock struck seven o'clock, at which point Dan would need me to take over kid duties so he could get himself to work.

Instead of relishing my two hours of freedom, I did what I promised myself I would not do when I set the alarm and turned out the light the night before. I drew my light-blocking curtains a little tighter, crawled into our warm bed, tucked the covers up to my chin, held my pillow against my body, and fell back to sleep, as I am wont to do.

As I drifted back into dreamland, I made myself a promise. I would not wake up two hours later and hate myself for being a lazy slob and sleeping when I could have been doing real things, especially exercising, because I have an admittedly irrational expectation that the baby weight needs to disappear as of yesterday. Instead, I would wake two hours later and be as kind to myself as I would be to a friend who was in the same position I was.

I would tell my friend, "Are you nuts!? You lost all the weight from your first pregnancy and you will do it this time too, but you shouldn't expect it to happen in less than two months. Cut yourself a break. You have a SEVEN-WEEK-OLD BABY."

I would tell my friend, "Yes, it is awesome that your baby pretty much slept through the night, but one night of decent sleep doesn't make up for seven weeks of crappy sleep."

I would tell my friend, "You have a lot on your plate right now. It's OK if your blog isn't updated."

I would tell my friend, "Be honest. You nursed the same cup of coffee all morning and into the afternoon before you even had one kid. That cup of morning coffee, enjoyed while still hot, has always been nothing more than a fantasy."

When I rose around 7 a.m., I felt rested. I wasn't exactly feeling like "Hurray for the day!" (to borrow a phrase from Sweet Pea). Yes, I had failed at the first order of business, the simple task of waking up at the desired time. But I wouldn't hate a friend or consider her a sloth just for shutting the alarm clock off at five after getting up with a baby before dawn.

We all know the Golden Rule: Do unto others as you would have them do unto you. It's not that hard to be nice to other people, really. Why is it sometimes so much harder to be nice to one's self?

So here is my Bizarro World Version of the Golden Rule: Do unto yourself as you would do unto others. I promise to be more mindful of it.

75

It Gets Easier

I OVERHEARD THE only dad in Sweet Pea's swim lesson mention something about a baby at home in between blowing bubbles and practicing reaching and pulling.

"We have a baby at home too." I offered.

"How old?" he asked.

"Four months. What about you?"

"Three days."

I smiled and offered congratulations.

"Does it get easier?" I could sense desperation in the way he asked. I would have embraced him in a hug if we weren't in the pool with our toddlers. And maybe if I knew his name.

"Um...eventually. A little. No. Sort of, yes. Yes, it definitely does. Gradually. I'd recommend keeping a flask full of whiskey in your swim trunks pocket." I didn't really say the part about the whiskey.

Everyone tells you to sleep while you can, have sex while you can, go out to dinner while you can, enjoy wearing something other than spit-up-stained yoga pants before you have your first baby.

As far as advice on having a toddler and a new baby… I only remember my mom quietly telling me, "It's going to be a hard year." I don't remember if that was before or after I collapsed in a pile of tears just before she and my dad left for the airport when the baby was two weeks old.

Now that Lady Bug is four months old, life is becoming marginally easier. Maybe it's only because after an entire summer and part of the fall, we are that many more days away from the time when we were a family of three. With every day that passes, being a family of four is gradually becoming our new normal. It doesn't hurt that my face is 95 percent healed. (I was diagnosed with Bell's palsy when Lady Bug was ten days old. Talk about a shitty postpartum.)

I hate to sound like an ungrateful little shit. I really try to think about—even when both kids are crowded onto my lap, Lady Bug screaming for a boob and Sweet Pea crying because she's two and a half and it could be anything—how lucky I am to have two healthy kids, a roof over our heads, and a husband who is truly a partner. At least once a day, usually around 5 p.m., when everyone is cranky and hungry and I'm trying to make dinner, I take a deep breath and remember that everything I have is everything I ever wanted.

But still. It really sucked to discover that half of my face was drooping like I'd had a stroke. And I'm not trying to minimize the experience of having a stroke. I'm just saying I looked *that bad*. Worse, there was no way to know how long it would take my face to get better or if it would ever get back to normal. For weeks, it was an effort to talk, to chew, to drink. Forget about smiling. One half of my face smiled and the other half didn't. It was 100 percent creepy looking. On the upside, being so self-conscious about my smile made me acutely aware of who in my life really makes me smile.

I had just given birth, my belly was like an overflowing bowl of Jell-O, Sweet Pea was running, jumping, screaming, and stomping in the house (all new behaviors), my limited free time was suddenly slashed in half, breastfeeding was a disaster (that experience deserves its own story), I went from the exhaustion of pregnancy to the exhaustion of waking up multiple times a night with a newborn, and then my face decided not to work. Every time I felt sad, I remembered how grateful I was supposed to feel, and then I hated myself even more for still being sad and became sadder still.

Things got noticeably better around the six-week mark. That was when I was allowed to exercise. Obviously, exercise gives you endorphins (i.e., the good-mood hormones). Exercise is also a special time when I get to be alone, either breathing fresh air outside or zoning out on the treadmill while indulging in something useless on Netflix.

Since then, there have been flashes of better that come at random...

When Sweet Pea gave Lady Bug her doll.
When both kids were supposed to be napping but instead they were crying, and Dan told me to take an hour and go to the nearest coffee shop with my laptop.
When Lady Bug slept four hours in a row.
When I ran a seven-miler with some hill repeats mixed in.
When I hit send on my first home birth book newsletter.
When I discovered Sweet Pea "reading" to Lady Bug...

Yeah, it does get easier.

76

Sweet Reunion

YESTERDAY I RAN about four and a half miles outside. This wouldn't be noteworthy, ordinarily, except I've been injured for nearly two months, which meant I had to stop running. I recently tried running a few times, just a few miles here and a few miles there, and only on the treadmill so that if my hip bothered me I could stop immediately. There are worse things than sweating in my basement with an episode of *Parenthood*. Still, I longed to run outside. Up until today, the last time I ran outside was seven weeks ago, the Sunday after Thanksgiving.

Maybe it sounds obsessive and strange that I would know the exact day that I last ran, but it wouldn't be wholly inaccurate to say I'm obsessive about running and a little strange about...many things.

If you've ever been dumped and you were heartsick about it and you replayed all the events leading up to the breakup, asking yourself, *What did I do? What did I say? Was I too much? Was I not enough? Was it the way I pronounced "Jeter"?* then maybe you can understand why I remember that last run, and all the runs immediately preceding it, so clearly.

If you've ever replayed a thousand times in your mind's eye the last time you and your ex were together, shaking your head every time, bewildered, because at the time you had no idea it would be the last time, then maybe you can relate.

If you've ever kicked yourself for having taken your time together—especially that last time—for granted, treated it as if it were just like all the other times, and wished you'd not been so blind because then maybe, just maybe, you could have prevented it from crashing down all around you—it's a lot like that.

Yesterday morning, I sat on the edge of the bed and put on my favorite leggings, along with a base layer and my trusty black Brooks long-sleeve half-zip top. And even though I wanted to go out and run on the road, I also wanted to do anything but go out and run. I felt blah. The sky was low, flat, and gray. My mind was cloudy and my body felt heavy.

I'm very tired and I have been for months. Even though I didn't think I could withstand sleep training our second child, it has come to that. For the past few nights in a row, instead of waking twice a night to quickly feed her and go back to sleep, I have lain awake in the dark, listening to her cry while my heart breaks, my blood pressure rises, my hair grays, and the wrinkles burrow ever deeper into the skin around my eyes. Dan suggests every night that I sleep in the guest room, where the sound would be less intense, but for reasons I don't totally understand, I would rather hear exactly what she is doing, even if I'm committed to ignoring it. Like I said, I'm strange.

I had hoped against hope that Lady Bug would surprise us. Maybe, despite her mercurial disposition, she would learn to put herself to sleep easily in just three nights, as the books and even my sister suggested was a real possibility. We are not so lucky. I am still exhausted.

I stepped into the chilly air and, though my legs felt like lead, I took a step. And then another. And another and another and another, until I forgot that I was tired. I forgot that I didn't really want to do this. I forgot about how badly I wanted a cup of coffee (or three). It was just me and the road, the sky, footstep after footstep. I like zoning out on my treadmill, but nothing will ever take the place of fixing my gaze on the mountains and breathing in the fresh air.

When I returned home, a layer of moisture lined my forehead where my hat had rested, and sweat lined the edges of my sports bra. My mind was clear and my heart was light. My world felt right again.

If your beloved has ever wrapped you up in the warmest, tightest embrace after a long time apart, and you nestled into his chest and took a deep, long breath of his familiar scent and you felt like you were home again, then you know what I'm talking about.

© Carrie Young

Pam Moore is a writer, mother, runner, and speaker. She writes about parenting, fitness, and life with her two kids, husband, and backyard chickens in Boulder, Colorado, at Whatevsblog.com, where she has been blogging since 2007. Her writing has appeared on websites including Huffington Post, Scary Mommy, Mamalode, and more. She dreams of completing everything on her to do list and qualifying for the Boston Marathon.

Twitter @PamMooreWriter
Facebook facebook.com/whatevsblog

www.ingramcontent.com/pod-product-compliance
Lightning Source LLC
Chambersburg PA
CBHW020610300426
44113CB00007B/586